Kansas

● Lorene White

● The Coens
■ ELKHART

aroline Henderson
●
● Boots McCoy   ● Dorothy Kleffman   ● Pauline Hodges   ● Wayne Lewis

● Imogene Glover   ■   ● Virginia Frantz
        GUYMON
● The Foresters

Trixie Travis
Brown
■
FOLLETT

Oklahoma

Texas

Tex Pace ●

Pauline Durrett Robertson
■ AMARILLO

THE DUST BOWL

*It was a decade-long natural catastrophe of biblical proportions—*when the skies refused their rains; when plagues of grasshoppers and swarms of rabbits descended on parched fields; when bewildered families huddled in darkened rooms while angry winds shook their homes, pillars of dust choked out the mid-day sun, and the land itself—the soil they had depended upon for their survival and counted on for their prosperity—turned against them with a lethal vengeance.

It was the worst man-made ecological disaster in American history— when the irresistible promise of easy money and the heedless actions of thousands of individuals, encouraged by their government, resulted in a collective tragedy that nearly swept away the breadbasket of the nation.

It was an epic of human pain and suffering—
when normally self-reliant fathers found themselves unable to provide for their families; when even the most vigilant mothers were unable to keep the dirt that invaded their houses from killing their children; when thousands of desperate Americans were torn from their homes and forced onto the road in an exodus unlike anything the United States has ever seen.

But the story of the Dust Bowl is also the story of heroic perseverance— of a resilient people who, against all odds, somehow managed to endure one unimaginable hardship after another to hold onto their lives, their land, and the ones they loved.

Copyright © 2012 by The Dust Bowl Film Project, LLC.

All rights reserved. No part of this book may be reproduced in any form without written permission from the publisher.

Page 219 constitutes a continuation of the copyright page.

Library of Congress Cataloging-in-Publication Data:

Duncan, Dayton.

  The Dust Bowl : an illustrated history / by Dayton Duncan; with a preface by Ken Burns; picture research by Aileen Silverstone and Susan Shumaker.

      pages cm.

  "Based on a film by Ken Burns, produced by Dayton Duncan, Ken Burns, and Julie Dunfey, written by Dayton Duncan."

  Includes bibliographical references and index.

  ISBN 978-1-4521-0794-3

1. Dust Bowl Era, 1931-1939. 2. Depressions—1929—Great Plains. 3. Great Plains—History—20th century. 4. Great Plains—Social conditions—20th century. 5. Droughts—Great Plains—History—20th century. 6. Farmers—Great Plains—Social conditions—20th century. I. Title.

F595.D93 2012
978'.032--dc23

2011052371

Manufactured in China

Designed by Suzanne M. LaGasa
Typeset in Caslon

10 9 8 7 6 5 4 3 2 1

Chronicle Books LLC
680 Second Street
San Francisco, California 94107
www.chroniclebooks.com

Endsheet image:

A dust storm bears down on the town of Darrouzett, Texas.

Preceding pages:

A dust storm descends on a solitary farmstead, 1935.

A Texas farmer attacks a sand dune with his team of horses and a drag pole.

Three Kansas children head for school wearing goggles and home-made dust masks.

A man struggles against a sandstorm in the Texas Panhandle.

Following page:
Two chickens head for cover near Ulysses, Kansas.

THE DUST BOWL

AN ILLUSTRATED HISTORY

BY **DAYTON DUNCAN**
BASED ON A FILM BY **KEN BURNS**

Produced by **Dayton Duncan, Ken Burns,** and **Julie Dunfey**
Written by **Dayton Duncan**

With a preface by **Ken Burns**

Picture research by **Aileen Silverstone** and **Susan Shumaker**

CHRONICLE BOOKS
SAN FRANCISCO

CONTENTS

LISTENING TO THE LAND

That country was so flat, you know. You could see for just miles. And they used to say that there wasn't a fence between there and the North Pole.

The grass was buffalo grass, and it was so good—it was unbelievable, it was so thick. God, it was good grass country. Man, it was perfect.

—Robert "Boots" McCoy
Texas County, Oklahoma

FOR A TRAVELER DRIVING SOUTH DOWN US 385/287 through the flat relentless expanses of first Prowers and then Baca County, Colorado, in the southeastern corner of that state, heading toward Oklahoma and the geographical heart of the ten-year disaster known as the Dust Bowl, it is impossible not to notice the relative stability and even peace of the landscape. Part of it is irrigation, of course, the modern wells and the giant-wheeled watering machines that suck up and distribute the scarcest commodity on the southern Plains.

Passing through Campo, the last town in Colorado, that landscape of immense farms and pasturage changes. One is near the center of the Comanche National Grassland, part of an immense federal effort starting in the 1930s to save the land that was once blowing away, convincing farmers to abandon the questionable agriculture practices that had for decades compelled the frantic human effort—and suffering—there, and return it to its natural state. The cottonwoods, willows, and locusts seem forlorn and sometimes bent, on guard, it almost seems, against the memory of forces once unleashed there, perhaps to come again.

A constant breeze stirs everything. Every green thing, the grasses, the thistles, the sagebrush (the "fag end of vegetable creation," Mark Twain once called it) are all in perpetual frantic animation, like the jerky, spastic motion of an old silent movie. Periodic crosses in the ditches just off the highway memorialize momentary mistakes at 75 miles per hour.

A scene along Highway 51 in Baca County, Colorado, in the 1930s.

Leaving the relative lushness, if that is what can be said of it, of Baca County and entering Cimarron Country—No Man's Land it was once called, at the extreme western end of the Oklahoma Panhandle—you realize you must be in a desert. Is it? Was it? Will it always be? Dead cottonwoods line the banks of the near bone-dry bed of the Cimarron River that, one is assured later, *does* run wet some of the time. Dust devils dance off to the left and then the right, innocent playful reminders of the devastating plagues that once beset this place.

Two daughters and their worried father, 1938.

It is a postapocalyptic world. Something happened here, and it is hard to even imagine agriculture ever thriving in this dryness—or a mountain range of dust coming at you, threatening everyone and everything dear to you. The first rise in miles is just a tumbledown butte, where whitewashed rocks, painted and arranged by the hands of still unseen humans, advertise St. Paul's Methodist Church down the road in the once dishonestly named Boise City.

But over a rise and beyond a graceful arcing bend in the blacktop, green fields suddenly stretch out as far as the eye can see and the landscape returns once again to flatness. Beautiful crops of grass and wheat, even high-maintenance corn (thanks to those giant water "walkers" that overrule the usual poor odds of moisture) unfold, which then just as fast yield to grazing land and weeds and back to cultivated land again. Farm buildings announce human habitation. The pickups pass with increasing frequency, their drivers waving in the custom of the Plains, a gesture of genuine friendliness that mitigates and helps to abolish the genuine loneliness of the mind-numbing distances required to do almost everything: shop, go to school, get to the hospital. The car radio anxiously cycles and searches and finds only one FM station, KJIL (Jesus Is Lord), where even the commercials earnestly cite scripture, and the conversation that day, without a hint of irony, is a "scientific" defense of the great biblical flood that washed away all but one human family. Out in the vast emptiness, any traveler might find comfort in its certainty and companionship.

The outskirts of Boise City reveal a nearly abandoned airfield and a now defunct lumberyard. Signs for 4-H and FFA optimistically still recruit. Listing wooden billboards celebrate an even earlier era, but the faded images of dinosaurs on them only evoke extinction. Grass-covered mounds betray but can't really hide the sand dunes that formed unexpectedly more than seventy-five years ago.

In the center of Boise City, the Cimarron County Courthouse is squeezed into the middle of what is no longer an expansive town square, but a traffic circle that rudely receives the jumble of national highways that seem to abruptly converge from all directions, and then just as quickly spins them all off again on new trajectories: to Clayton, New Mexico; Dalhart and Amarillo, Texas; Guymon, Oklahoma; Elkhart, Kansas; even back to Campo and Springfield in Colorado, and other parts of No Man's Land, the five-state congregation that would eventually be called the Dust Bowl.

On the surface, Boise City is a hard luck town. There are now, at least, trees, but weeds sprout from the doorways of the old shops on the main commercial street. The flourishing businesses are the gas stations and convenience stores that hurry travelers, both local and foreign, along. On the side streets, neat new small homes compete with old shacks that somehow survived the hard times but are now no longer fit for occupation. Across from St. Paul's Methodist Church is the small bungalow that was once the Shaw Funeral Home, where, on a Sunday in the spring of 1935, its proprietors prepared to bury the youngest and the oldest of their clan.

South of town, on the road to Clayton, proud new grain elevators, the skyscrapers of the prairie, still receive the precious output of the seemingly healthy farms. The Soil Conservation Service, which arrived in the midst of the troubles like the cavalry that rescued the pioneers of the Santa Fe Trail (whose telltale ruts can be found just north of town), still has an office here. A four-locomotive (two pulling, two pushing) Burlington Northern and Santa Fe Railway train carries only coal in a hundred cars as it passes an old grain elevator, old enough to have stored the wheat from those good years of the late 1920s and overflowed with the near worthless grain when the market collapsed just a few seasons later. Then the rains had stopped and the dusters started to blot out the sun.

It's hard to appreciate the size of things in the vastness of the Great Plains, a place most of us experience only from the window of a plane. Cities—and modern travel—tend to contract and focus our sense of space, but out in No Man's Land, in the relatively, for them, short distances between small villages, there is room for three Manhattans—or maybe even ten. Cities and suburbs permit us sweeping generalizations about people and human behavior, while the randomness and isolation of rural life defy our preconceptions, or perhaps oversimplify them, missing the essential value gleaned from their age-old struggle with the land.

> *Let me tell you how it was. I don't care who describes it to you, nobody can tell it any worse than what it was. And no one exaggerates; there is no way for it to be exaggerated. It was that bad.*
>
> —*Don Wells*
> *Cimarron County, Oklahoma*

FOR SEVERAL YEARS NOW we have been engaged in making a documentary film on the history of the Dust Bowl of the 1930s—the greatest man-made ecological disaster in American history—struggling to understand its very human causes, what it was like to live and survive in that inhospitable landscape that eventually killed not only people's crops and cattle but their children; why some stayed and some left; how humans tried to reverse what seemed to be irreversible; how the crisis abated and how the painful hard lessons were quickly forgotten.

Though the most compelling "characters" in this drama may be the terrifying black blizzards, the dust storms—sometimes a hundred of them in a single year—that tortured and destroyed much of the southern Plains, it was the people, the survivors that interested us most. And so our two-part, four-hour documentary film series is an oral history, filled with the commentary of two dozen individuals who witnessed this calamity firsthand, whose family struggles reveal an essential American character, a story of heroic and harrowing perseverance.

They are, in turn, aided by the participation of a handful of historians, both local and national, who provide, we believe, valuable context, helping us understand that this is also the story of the roles and limits of government, and ultimately that it is a morality tale about our relationship to the land that sustains us—a lesson we ignore at our peril. In this sense, the themes and meanings of the Dust Bowl are as contemporary and as vital as any history we have ever undertaken.

"Listen to the land," the Pulitzer Prize–winning writer Timothy Egan told us. "Don't try to put things in place there that don't belong there. The Dust Bowl wasn't a natural disaster—it was a human disaster. We didn't set out and say, 'Let's ruin the second greatest ecosystem in North America.' It was a result of a whole bunch of things that are just innate to human beings. It's a classic tale of human beings pushing too hard against nature, and nature pushing back." He was describing events that took place three-quarters of a century ago; he could just as easily have been talking about yesterday. Or tomorrow.

As an outgrowth of our documentary project, this book is a way to expand or include stories shortened or cut out altogether by the often merciless necessities of filmmaking. As we finished our film and wrote this book, we couldn't help but notice that the southern Plains were again in the midst of a devastating drought, that the story we were telling about personal dramas played out decades ago was perhaps being relived again. But the story we are trying to tell documents a full decade of human pain and environmental degradation, a time when dust from No Man's Land coated the desk of the President of the United States in Washington, D.C. If the current economic recession also suggests comparisons to the Great Depression, the cataclysm that cruelly superimposed itself over the Dust Bowl, they are also only superficial; no animals in our zoos are being shot now and their meat distributed to the poor, as they were during the time of the Depression and the Dust Bowl.

There are other misconceptions. Say "Dust Bowl" and most people think of John Steinbeck's powerful story of the Joad family in *The Grapes of Wrath*. They may have been "Okies," the derogatory name given to all those who abandoned the Plains for California and elsewhere for a second chance, but the Joads were actually tenant farmers from Sallisaw, in far eastern Oklahoma near the border with Arkansas, forced from the land they worked on for *others* by drought, to be sure, but also the Depression.

Out in the far western reaches of the state, those most affected by the ravages of the Dust Bowl were landowners, forced to confront agonizing realities of foreclosure and forfeiture as well as eviction, forced to confront a disease that capriciously killed their loved ones as well as the crushing poverty of hard economic times, and finally forced to confront the fact that their very presence on the land had helped create the disaster in the first place.

There's no way you can control it. It's comin' and there's nothing you can do about it. I guess it would be kind of a hopeless feeling, because you knew there was no way that you were going to control that wind and that dirt.

It was going to come in your house; it was going to come in any place that it could get in. You were not in control. You were caught up in the middle of this, and there was no way you could get out.

—*Dorothy Sturdivan Kleffman*
Texas County, Oklahoma

A farmer sharpens his scythe as clouds gather.

WE TRIED TO TELL OUR STORY in a variety of familiar ways for us—a third-person narration that provides facts and a running chronology, the commentary of historians, live modern cinematography gathered in every season and from every time of day and night, rare archival photographs and footage culled from dozens and dozens of sources around the country, and period and contemporary music. But this film, and now this book, benefit most from our witnesses.

These survivors, most of them now in their eighties and some in their nineties, lived through this horror, and their memories are as vivid as if it had all happened a moment ago. They made the film different from nearly all others we have worked on, and their words have enriched the narrative of this book. They are a remarkable cast of characters who as children lived through unbelievable hardship. This was the last chance for many of them to record their stories in their own words.

To their unforgettable recountings, we have also added first-person quotes from a handful of memorable historical characters, whose letters and journals add yet another dimension to this epic human tragedy, a tragedy as relevant today as when those sandstorms and dust storms blasted the hopes of thousands of our fellow citizens. The backbone of our narrative, in fact, is the story of Caroline Boa Henderson, who arrived in No Man's Land as a hopeful homesteader and then eloquently chronicled the unrelenting difficulties she and her husband, Will, experienced on the plot of ground they called home. Our account of this extraordinary and important moment in American history begins and ends with Caroline's voice speaking to us across the years. "To prepare the ground as well as we may, to sow our seeds, to cultivate and care for, that is our part," she reminds us. "Yet how difficult it is for some of us to learn that the results we must leave to the great silent unseen forces of Nature, whether the crop be corn or character."

Back in the wide open, horizon-stretching infiniteness of things in No Man's Land, the human overlay of roads and fields, power lines and silos, oil and gas wells, windmills and homes is impressive, evidence of decades of striving, of trying to ignore the fact that this agricultural region still has near desert–level precipitation. A small farm road, High Lonesome Lane of all names, leads the traveler back to the highway, and then north, back into Boise City—ground zero for the stories and lessons of the Dust Bowl. In the northeast corner of the busy, long haul truck–filled, diesel-fumed traffic circle posing as a town square, the crude Cimarron County Events sign, angled arbitrarily on a sidewalk in front of a closed business, lists three things. The first alerts citizens to the blood drive at the Christian Church. The next advertises that athletic physicals for the Wildcats will take place at the health clinic. The last message is the enduring one for this town and area: PRAY FOR RAIN.

—KEN BURNS
Walpole, New Hampshire

Chapter 1

THE GREAT PLOW UP

April 28, 1908

Here I am, away out in that narrow strip of Oklahoma between Kansas and the Panhandle of Texas, "holding down" one of the prettiest claims . . .

I wish you could see this wide, free, western country, with its real stretches of almost level prairie, covered with the thick, short buffalo grass, the marvelous glory of its sunrises and sunsets, the brilliancy of its star lit sky at night.

. . .Out here in this wilderness has come to me the very greatest and sweetest and most hopeful happiness of all my life.

—Caroline Henderson

FROM THE TIME SHE WAS A YOUNG girl, Caroline Boa Henderson had dreamed of having a piece of land she could call her own. The intelligent and adventurous eldest child of a prosperous Iowa farm family, she had gone east to study languages and literature at Mount Holyoke College, where her senior class prophecy predicted that her future would be found "somewhere on a western ranch." In 1907, the year of Oklahoma's statehood, she followed that dream to a narrow strip of Oklahoma that bordered four other states—Kansas, Texas, New Mexico, and Colorado—which had only recently been opened for settlement, a formerly lawless and ungovernable place called No Man's Land. There she took a job teaching school near the settlement of Eva, staked out a homestead claim on 160 acres, and moved into a one-room shack, 14 by 16 feet, which she dubbed her "castle."

A year later, she married Will Henderson, a lanky Kansas cowboy she had met when he showed up with the crew she hired to dig her well. They soon had a daughter, Eleanor, and Will built an addition to their home. Their work brought them closer to fulfilling the requirements of the Homestead Act and gaining title to the farm, where they raised broomcorn, millet, and maize, turkeys, chickens, and a few cattle. They put what little cash they earned into improvements, particularly a new windmill to draw up water for their animals, house, and half-acre garden. To bring in extra money, Caroline began submitting articles about life on the Plains to magazines: the *Practical Farmer*, where a $2 fee for a short piece describing their broomcorn crop earned the Hendersons more money than the crop itself; *Ladies' World*, where her monthly column, "Homestead Lady," became its most popular feature; and the *Atlantic Monthly*, the nation's most prestigious publication.

She wrote mostly about the everyday occurrences on her farm: nurturing a small grove of locust trees to provide shade or raising a flock of turkeys for a modest profit, preparing an entirely homegrown Thanksgiving dinner or attending to the birth of a calf, the simple joys of reading books aloud with Will in the evening or taking Sunday morning walks with him "through our fields, noticing the growth of each separate planting, our hearts full of thankfulness for the hope of it and for everything." She also wrote with surprising honesty about her own struggles against depression, her critiques of churchgoers whose religion focused only on a belief in heaven, her nagging fears of failing at her self-appointed mission as a woman homesteader, or how much the weather and the

After graduating from Mount Holyoke College in 1901 (top, left), Caroline Boa Henderson moved to the Oklahoma Panhandle and built her "castle" (top, right). By 1911 she and her husband, Will (cutting broomcorn, above, while daughter Eleanor watches), were expanding the homestead.

Preceding pages:
A herd of bison grazes on the southern Plains; the buffalo grass sustained them through dry years as well as wet cycles.

natural world influenced her outlook on life. And she constantly infused her articles with lyrical descriptions of the sweeping, starkly beautiful land that was steadily exerting a powerful hold on her: "the whiteness of our Monday's washing against . . . the blue of the summer sky, the drifting of cloud-shadows over a field of ripening wheat . . . [and] the hush of early morning broken by the first bird's song."

Although she harbored great ambitions of doing as well on her Oklahoma homestead as her father had on his Iowa farm, Caroline understood that wresting a living from the land was a risky undertaking on the southern Plains, a region of infrequent rains, few trees, and constant winds. "Our farming here," she wrote a college classmate back East, "often reminds me of the man who, when asked to embark upon some rather doubtful business venture, replied that if he wanted to gamble he would prefer roulette, I believe, where the chances were only 32-to-1 against him."

In that joking assessment of her odds, Caroline Henderson was much more optimistic than the first white Americans to explore the area. In 1806, on a western expedition dispatched by President Thomas Jefferson, Lieutenant Zebulon Pike reported seeing "not a stick of timber," and predicted that the Plains "may become in time equally celebrated as the sandy deserts of Africa." More than a decade later, the leader of another U.S. Army exploration, Major Stephen Long, wrote "Great Desert" across his official map of the region and ominously described it as "almost wholly unfit for cultivation, and of course, uninhabitable by a people depending upon agriculture for subsistence."

But the Plains Indians considered it home. The short grasses that covered the treeless expanse sent tangled roots five feet below the ground, forming a dense sod that could withstand the region's unfailingly recurrent droughts and violent weather extremes—nourishing deer, antelope, jackrabbits, and the vast herds of buffalo that grazed in numbers beyond counting. It was an evolutionary adaptation, worked out over millions of years, which environmental historian Donald Worster has called "nature's winning design." The Native Americans, in turn, survived and

prospered by adapting too. Whether they were nomadic hunters of the abundant game or established farmers, they reconciled their cultures to the environment as it was.

By the late 1800s, all that changed. The bison were slaughtered by market hunters and the Indians were driven onto reservations. Cattlemen took over, in what was called the Beef Bonanza. But severe winters in the 1880s killed off their herds, and the Beef Bonanza went bust.

Homesteaders came next, swarming onto land once considered unsuitable for crops because it averaged less than 20 inches of rain a year. Boosters and unscrupulous promoters promised that the very act of farming would increase the precipitation: "Rain follows the plow," they said. A six-year drought in the 1890s proved them wrong. Dust storms devastated livestock and crops. Counties that had tripled and quadrupled in population in less than a decade emptied just as quickly. Wagons emblazoned with In God We Trusted,

In Kansas We Busted began streaming east, filled with ruined settlers. "West of Junction City there is no Sunday," one dejected homesteader said on his retreat from the Plains, "and west of Salina, there is no God."

Then, in the early part of the twentieth century, Congress enlarged the original Homestead Act, enticing farmers to settle on some of the last available sections of arable public land in the nation. Most of the newcomers, nearly all of them white, came from Europe, where land was unavailable, and from parts of the United States where it was too expensive. "For the first time in their family history, most of these people owned a piece of dirt," said author and journalist Timothy Egan. "They were Scots-Irish who'd been kicked around the old Confederacy. They were Germans from the Russian steppe. They were Latinos who came up from the South. They were folks that had never owned anything." In the southern Plains, many of them converged on the area where Caroline Henderson

ENDLESS AND UNPLOWED: An early settler sits on the flat expanse of buffalo grass in southwestern Kansas, 1897.

had staked her future. In No Man's Land alone, 32,000 new settlers arrived by 1907, 16,448 of them in the freshly created Texas County, the place that Caroline now considered home.

Like their neighbors, the Hendersons considered themselves "next year" people, ready to face the myriad adversities of pioneering in a place so vulnerable to wild shifts of weather, always clinging to the hope embodied in the three words that defined their existence: "if it rains." Caroline could not help projecting her own feelings and desires onto the weather that determined their success or failure, as she explained in *Ladies' World*:

> Many a time I have found myself tired out from having tried unconsciously and without success to bring the distant rainclouds nearer, to water our fields. Often I have felt as if the responsibility for averting a blizzard or a hailstorm rested upon me, and I seemed actually to be struggling against some great overpowering weight.
>
> I am beginning to see how worse than useless is this exaggerated feeling of one's own responsibility; to understand a little the thought of someone who wrote long ago, "He that observeth the wind shall not sow, and he that regardeth the clouds shall not reap."

IN THE MID-1910S, THE SOUTHERN Plains entered a relatively wet period, and the pace of settlement quickened. Real estate syndicates began buying big ranches for $5 an acre and carving them up into smaller parcels for sale at three times the price. Railroad companies did the same thing with the huge tracts they had been given by the government. Special excursion trains brought prospective buyers to the region by the thousands, as salesmen quoted favorable statistics about the amount of rainfall and productivity of the soil. None other than the former chancellor of the University of Kansas, they were told, had determined that the climate was undergoing a permanent shift: precipitation was increasing, and the winds were slowing down. Another expert opined that removing the cover of prairie grasses allowed more rainfall to penetrate the soil.

"NEXT YEAR" PEOPLE: The Agston family put on their best clothes (above) for a portrait in front of the wooden entrance to their earthen dugout near Boise City, Oklahoma. Near the town of Gate, another proud family (right) used sod bricks to elevate their ceiling at least partially aboveground. Wayne Lewis's father purchased this house and property.

Towers sprang up overnight. One of the first groups to buy land near Guymon, Oklahoma, south of Caroline and Will Henderson's homestead, simply got off a train, climbed to the top of the railroad's cattle pens, and picked out their sites. Farther west, in nearby Cimarron County, the developers of Boise City sold house lots to buyers who didn't even bother to come for an inspection. The city's very name—from *bois*, French for "wood" or "forest"—was a deliberate deception. There were no trees in Boise City. Nor were there any of the other things the promoters had promised in their advertisements: artesian wells, a bustling business district, and broad streets lined by stately elms and maples with fancy houses being built in their shade. The promises were so overblown, in fact, that the developers were later convicted in federal court of real estate fraud; one of them died in a penitentiary while serving out his sentence.

"Oklahoma," one railroad brochure bragged, "grows better cattle than Texas, better corn than Kansas or Minnesota, better cotton than Mississippi or Alabama, better fruit than Arkansas or Missouri, better potatoes than Colorado, better peanuts than Virginia or North Carolina, better horses than Kentucky, better wool and mutton than Ohio, [and] better swine than anywhere."

But increasingly, in western Oklahoma and throughout the southern Plains, the focus was almost exclusively on wheat. With the outbreak of World War I in Europe, German blockades cut off access to Russian wheat. In the United States, farmers mobilized to feed the Allies. Under the slogan, "Wheat will win the war," Washington set the price of wheat at a minimum of $2 a bushel, double the previous rate. In five years, more than 11 million acres of virgin soil were plowed for the first time: An area twice the size of New Jersey was converted from native pasture to wheat fields.

When the war ended, wheat prices declined. But the plowing and planting only increased. There was still good money to be made and lots of cheap or free land

still available on what the federal government had declared "the last frontier of agriculture." Fueled by the desire to get ahead in life on land that was theirs and theirs alone, the "next year" people looked toward a future in which the skies would continue watering their crops, prices would hold steady, and their families would prosper.

No one seemed immune from the optimism filling the air. It was part of the oxygen everyone breathed.

Close to the Hendersons in Texas County, Imogene Davison Glover's parents had moved into a three-room house on land where her father raised turkeys and cattle— and then wheat. More than eighty years later, she could still remember running barefoot behind his plow as it turned the sod, creating a deep furrow of cool, damp earth. "He was a gambler," Imogene said of her father, "but I think every farmer's a gambler. They have to gamble that what they're putting into the ground is going to grow and produce and they'll get better off. They thought they'd all get rich or wealthy. There was no reason not to think so at that time."

A little to the east, in neighboring Beaver County, Oklahoma, Pauline Arnett Hodges's parents had started a new life

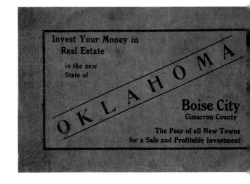

Brochures touted Boise City as a thriving town of the future (above), but when it officially opened in 1908 (top), even its name—from the French for "forest"—proved patently fraudulent.

with bright expectations. "I think my parents were pretty typical of that time," she said. "They came out from Missouri in 1921 and became wheat farmers. My father said he'd had forty acres in Missouri, but he could have one hundred and sixty acres out in Beaver County. And he just thought that was wonderful. His idea of farming was what he had done in Missouri, which was plow the land up and everything would grow and we'll get rainfall. And for about ten years he had bumper wheat crops and did very well."

Just across the state line, in southwestern Kansas, the lure of cheap land and the chance to make money on wheat

Imogene Davison Glover (below, back left) loved to scamper behind her father's plow as he turned the sod for the first time.

persuaded Lorene Delay White's father to leave his rented farm near Dodge City and relocate his family to Stanton County. Lorene, age ten, was against it. She enjoyed living near her grandparents and feared that moving more than 100 miles away meant she would never see them again. But her father prevailed, and when he brought the family to their new farm, she cried for days. "I had never seen any place so flat and so devoid of trees in all my life," Lorene recalled. "There was nothing on our land. It was just a piece of flat ground that dad had plowed. I thought, 'oh, if we could just have trees.'" There was no house, either, just a large chicken coop under construction, which was soon converted into a three-room dwelling for the Delays and their four children. Lorene, the oldest, quickly adapted to her new surroundings. "It's real funny," she said, "but as much as I didn't want to come, in a short while I was having the time of my life. We had neighbors that had kids my age and that was something we hadn't had. So that made me happy. And I soon grew to love the country and still do."

Not far from the Delays, in Morton County, Kansas, Edgar Coen had taken over 160 acres from a homesteader who had been run off by cowboys just before the war. At first, he moved his wife, Rena, and their five-month-old son into a one-room 10-by-12-foot dugout he had carved out of the soil. It extended only 2½ feet above the ground, with small windows to let in a little light. Its "front door" was a cellar door that opened into the cave-like space, its dirt walls were covered with canvas and its dirt floor by a rug. "It's a shame, dear," Edgar told his bride, "to bring you to a place like this." As the family grew, Edgar added more rooms, then an above-ground entrance big enough to double as a kitchen. By scrimping and saving, he was able to acquire 160 more acres and build a barn for his livestock. On weekends, friends from the surrounding countryside would help Rena move her piano from the dugout to the hayloft of the big barn, where the Coens hosted square dances that would last

Edgar and Rena Coen (top, left) looked forward to a bigger family and a house aboveground. Sam and Nora Beck (above) hoped to move from his brother's land to a farm of their own.

all night. "It was a happy life," Dale Coen, one of the boys, remembered. "We had pretty good crops. Dad was really excited about the way they were making progress there on the claim. And he was going to build a home."

South of the Coens, in Cimarron County, Oklahoma, Sam Beck didn't have enough money to buy a farm. But his brother, a farmer in central Kansas, had purchased a 640-acre section of land near the town of Wheeless, west of Boise City, and told Sam he could farm it until he made enough to get his own place. In 1928, Sam brought his wife, Nora, and their two children to their new home. Clarence, their son, said, "They thought they were going to make money, enjoy a reasonably good life, and eventually maybe even own a farm of their own. Any thoughts toward wealth were always about owning more land. That was everybody's expectation: 'If I can just make it, I can buy another one hundred and sixty or three hundred and twenty acres of land.' So their expectation was to own a place of their own and if possible to make it as big as possible."

All across the southern Plains, the story was the same, according to Pauline Arnett Hodges:

Wheat was just a bonanza, and everybody had good crops. Like a lot of folks I think [my parents] thought it would last forever. They plowed up every piece of land they could get ahold of. Some of it is quite good land. It's flat; it's sandy loam. Then there's land that's marginal. It didn't matter; they plowed it all up.

And the more wheat they raised, the more land they plowed up. And they bought more land, they bought more possessions, they bought new cars, and they lived quite well. They were able to acquire more land probably than they should have.

Modern machinery made wheat farming more efficient, and still profitable at prices of about $1 per bushel. Powerful gasoline tractors, pulling broad arrays of disc plows, turned the sod with ease. In previous years, farmers had used a plow called a lister, with a double moldboard with curved blades that split the soil in two directions and dug a deep furrow that caught and held blowing soil. Now, the most commonly used plow was called a one-way, which simply pulverized the top layer of soil, but was cheaper and tore through the sod at a faster rate,

An array of one-way plows converts the buffalo grass to a cultivated field in Caroline Henderson's home county in Oklahoma's No Man's Land.

reducing costs even more. At harvesttime, new machines called combines cut a farmer's costs in half and reduced labor time to a quarter of what it had once been using horses and field-workers.

Throughout the nation, farms were increasingly seen as food "factories," and winter wheat was particularly well suited to this new, more industrial model of agriculture. It didn't require as much cultivation and weeding as corn, and it didn't need the same care and feeding as cattle, hogs, or chickens. A farmer planted his seed in the fall and then essentially waited for early summer to harvest his crop. If the weather cooperated with adequate moisture, he could make a sizable amount of cash compared with other types of farming. One good wheat crop generated the equivalent return of ten years raising stock on the same amount of land. And the more land a farmer put into wheat, the bigger the potential payoff.

In 1926, Ida Watkins, who called herself the "wheat queen" of Haskell County, Kansas, claimed that her 2,000-acre farm returned a profit of $75,000—more than the salary of President Calvin Coolidge. Tales of such big profits brought droves of "suitcase farmers" into the region—city dwellers who came out and bought or leased large sections of land, much of it only marginally suitable for converting to crops. They would pay someone to plow the fields and plant the wheat, and then returned to their homes. The next summer, they hired crews to bring in their crop. Down in the Texas Panhandle, a Hollywood producer for the Fox Film Corporation bought 54 square miles of grassland and turned it all to wheat. He used a fleet of twenty-five combines to harvest half a million bushels of grain. His crews worked day and night, turning on lights when the sun went down.

Even if they shared some of the same dreams as the "suitcase farmers"—that the speculative bubble building around wheat would continue uninterrupted—the homesteaders viewed these outsiders with contempt. "They never set down roots or built homes or nothing," Floyd Coen said of them. "They would just come out, plow it up, sow it, go back home, and come out in the summer to harvest it. And they never added much to the community."

Oklahoma homesteader Caroline Henderson felt the same way:

The "suitcase farmers"—that is, insurance agents, preachers, real estate

men, and so forth, from cities near and far—have bet thousands of dollars upon rain, *or, in other words, have hired the preparation of large areas of land all around us which no longer represent the idea of* homes *at all, but just parts of a potential factory for the low-cost production of wheat*—if it rains.

In southeastern Colorado, John Crabill hoped to make a good life for himself and his family raising horses and cattle. But to get ahead, he took a job driving a tractor on other people's land, often working the night shift plowing fields. "And he knew at the time it was the wrong thing," his son, Calvin, said. "He knew that buffalo grass was the natural turf of that country and it was grazing country. But he would work many years as a plowman for these men doing wheat. He was really a stockman and he knew it was all wrong. And he paid the price for it later."

Crabill was not alone in his skepticism. "There were a lot of cattlemen who were very worried about this process," according to historian Donald Worster. "They'd always been suspicious of farmers anyway. But a lot of cattlemen said, 'This is not the way to handle this kind of land. We've been here for at least forty or fifty years. We've

been through booms and bust. We know how fragile this place is. This is not the way to go about it.' " To them, this was a *grassland*, and the sod should never have been turned. In the Texas Panhandle, near the town of Dalhart, a half-Anglo, half-Apache cowboy named Bam White explained it succinctly to his son. He picked up a piece of sod, freshly flipped by a plow, and declared: "Wrong side up."

But with the rain plentiful and the cash crop of wheat generating consistent profits, the doubters were easily ignored. Yields were averaging 13 bushels an acre. During the last five years of the 1920s alone, as wheat acreage expanded by 200 percent, another 5,260,000 acres of native grassland—an area the size of New Hampshire—was turned over on the southern Plains. "It's a very complex ecosystem that evolved over thousands of years," writer Timothy Egan said. "In less than a generation's time, they peeled the whole thing off."

The government acted as the principal cheerleader. "The soil," a federal agency confidently proclaimed, "is the one indestructible, immutable asset that the nation possesses. It is the one resource that cannot be exhausted, that cannot be used up." Texas County, Oklahoma, where Caroline Henderson lived, was singled out as the

Some Kansas farmers pause from the harvest, with their tractors and combines arrayed behind them.

most productive winter-wheat county in the nation. Even she could not help being caught up in the spell of the transformation she had witnessed since first filing for her homestead:

> *A few days ago I rode to the store for the mail. Coming home . . . I saw the whole country transformed in the sunset glow—all the brown prairie turned to gold. Little low buildings grouped about upward-reaching windmills made tiny specks upon a wide horizon, each telling of effort, sacrifice, aspiration.*
>
> *I could feel once more the lure of this great, lonely land, waiting with its stores of fertility all untouched for those who shall one day learn to meet its demands, to give to it their patient thought and labor.*

AMONG CAROLINE HENDERSON'S neighbors in Texas County was the family of Harry Forester, a pious, hardworking farmer with a third-grade education but grand ambitions. Born in Arkansas, the fourth of eleven children, he had grown up moving by covered wagon with his parents and siblings to a succession of central Texas farms, until an outbreak of malaria forced them to move once more, this time to the drier climate of the Panhandle. At age twenty-one, Forester struck off on his own, crossed into Oklahoma, and filed on a homestead in No Man's Land. The daughter of a neighboring farmer, Rose Cooksey, caught his eye, and in 1911, he wrote her a note: "I've just gotten a new buggy from Sears Roebuck. How about going for a ride with me after church?"

John Crabill, (below left, gathering Russian thistles with his son, Calvin), was skeptical about plowing up the rangeland, but Harry Forester (with bib overalls, below right) dreamed of bequeathing 640 acres of productive wheat land to each of his sons.

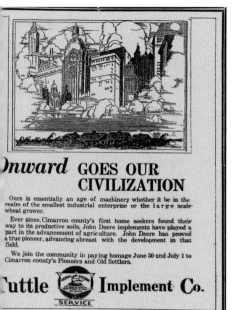

Even after the stock market crash of 1929, the residents of No Man's Land felt prosperous. Caroline Henderson (left) had an abundant garden. Boise City (right) had certainly grown in 20 years, but its boosters were still imagining bigger things for the future (above).

Before the year was out, they were married and immediately began a family.

As times improved, Forester's dreams expanded. He remembered hearing of a farmer in the Texas Panhandle whose profits from wheat made it possible to bequeath each of his sons a square mile of good land before he died. Harry Forester determined to do the same thing—a highly ambitious goal, because he now had nine children, and five of them were sons.

He got a job that paid decent wages running the dairy farm for the state college in Goodwell, Oklahoma, and moved his family into town, so his children could be better educated. Meanwhile, he continued growing wheat on his homestead. Then, to enlarge his holdings, in 1928 Forester leveraged the land he already owned with a mortgage to buy even more wheat-growing land near Boise City. "He had used all his property and all his lands and all he had accrued from 1906 to 1928," his youngest son, William, said. "Because of his dream he essentially put it all at risk. And ultimately it proved to be a bad time to make a move."

On October 29, 1929, a day that would be remembered as "Black Tuesday," the stock market crashed on Wall Street, puncturing a financial bubble that had been building throughout the 1920s. By the end of the year, the devastation had spread to other parts of the economy, throwing one and a half million Americans out of work. A year later, that number tripled, and the nation descended into the Great Depression.

Nearly 27,000 businesses failed, including 1,372 banks that took $3 billion in deposits down with them. In the summer of 1930, evictions in Philadelphia rose to 1,300 a month. In New York, destitute residents were being fed 85,000 meals a day in the city's 82 breadlines. Six thousand men were reduced to selling apples on street corners for a nickel apiece, hoping to clear a dollar for their day's effort. On one block of West Forty-Third Street, an observer counted 19 shoeshine stands, manned by bootblacks ranging from age sixteen to older than seventy.

But back in No Man's Land, the future still looked bright. Prospects for a new railroad line prompted the editor of the Boise City newspaper to proclaim, "Our ship is coming in—loaded with something for each us." An advertisement imagined a Manhattan-style skyline, with the prediction, "Soon you will have your own Empire State Building, right across from Kirby's Kash Grocery." The town of Liberal, Kansas, began planning for a new airport, and its country club completed a membership drive to build a new clubhouse. "No Slump for Us Yet," the *Liberal News* trumpeted across its front page. The southern Plains, the U.S. Chamber of Commerce declared, was now one of the most prosperous areas in the nation.

Most of what people knew about the misery gripping the rest of America, they learned from watching newsreels at the Palace Theater in Boise City or the Mission Theater in Dalhart, Texas. "The first two years," Pauline Arnett Hodges recalled, "they thought it didn't affect them, that it was back East, that [the Depression] was in Chicago, that it was in New York. It wasn't here. This won't happen to us." After harvesting his best crop ever in 1929, Imogene Davison Glover's father bought his first automobile, a brand-new Model T, and took his family on a vacation to New Mexico. "Everything was looking up," she said. "It was a great time."

In Morton County, Kansas, Edgar and Rena Coen now had six children—all of them boys. It was time, Edgar decided, to move out of the dugout. He hooked up his horses to an earthmoving scraper called a fresno and began excavating a large basement, with concrete walls he mixed and poured by hand, to serve as the foundation for the proper home he intended to provide his growing family.

In the Panhandle town of Follett, Texas, Trixie Travis Brown's father believed the time was right to start a new business. He and his father and brother opened a hardware store on Follett's main street. Then he moved his wife and two girls into a new house in town. "It was new. It was great," Trixie said. "Things seemed to be going well for my dad and for Grandpa."

But throughout the nation in the 1920s, as Europe's own agricultural economy recovered from its wartime devastation and America's "factory farms" expanded, an oversupply of virtually all farm commodities had been accumulating, pushing prices down and putting an economic squeeze on all farmers, especially those who had gone deeply into debt during the earlier boom. Between 1925 and 1926, the price of cotton had dropped from 17 cents to 9 cents a pound, then to 5 cents a pound five years later. So many cotton farmers were driven out of business that by the end of the 1920s, 61 percent of them in Oklahoma had become tenants, working someone else's land. Dairymen in Iowa became so frustrated by low milk prices, they blockaded the roads into Sioux City with telegraph poles and emptied the contents of milk trucks into the ditches. When a sheriff tried to intervene, they took away his badge and tossed it into a cornfield, along with his gun.

Wheat prices had started dropping, too: in 1930, to 70 cents a bushel. Pleas from President Herbert Hoover's Federal Farm Board for growers to reduce their acreage in wheat went unheeded. Instead, farmers decided, if they couldn't make as much money *per* bushel, they would simply harvest *more* bushels. So they plowed up more land—half a million more acres in the counties around No Man's Land. Even Ida Watkins, the Kansas "wheat queen," planted four times as many acres as she had five years earlier.

It snowed and rained that winter; and the spring of 1931 brought adequate moisture. By harvesttime, the winter wheat was shoulder-high, and farmers realized

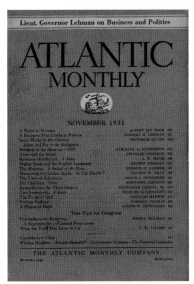

By 1931, Caroline and Will Henderson had a new tractor and combine for their bumper wheat crop (right), a new house with a small grove of planted trees (top), and Caroline's article, "Bringing in the Sheaves," was among those listed on the cover of the *Atlantic Monthly* (above).

In Follett, Texas, with local grain elevators already filled, the town's main street became the temporary storage location for the overwhelming wheat crop of 1931.

they had a bumper crop on their hands—a bonanza yield in terms of quality and quantity (an astonishing 17.7 bushels an acre in southwestern Kansas). Caroline Henderson described it for the *Atlantic Monthly* in an article entitled "Bringing in the Sheaves":

> *Early and late, from all directions, has resounded the hum of tractors and combines. Trucks have been hastening over the roads, carrying piled-up loads of bright, hard, full-kerneled wheat to granaries or elevators.*
>
> *Toward nightfall in the sunset glow the air has been luminous with the incandescent dust rising in a cloud about each moving combine. I have never seen a more beautiful harvest . . . one of the best wheat crops this country has ever produced in our twenty-four years of farming.*

Over the years, Caroline and Will had increased their holdings to 640 acres, a square mile. They had purchased mechanized equipment to replace their reliance on horses. ("What would my father think of our temerity in driving around our fields cutting and threshing all at one operation?" she marveled about their new combine. Caroline managed the combine, while their daughter, Eleanor, home from college, drove the tractor pulling it, and Will shoveled the threshed grain.) And they now had a new house, with a full basement, five rooms on the first floor, and a big unfinished room on the second. It had an indoor bathroom, but as yet no running water. And they had a telephone, serviced by a new company that had reached the rural parts of Texas County. Not only had they been able to send Eleanor to the University of Kansas, aiming for a medical degree, but Caroline had gone along with her for two years and, though now in her fifties, received a master's degree in literature. (Mother and daughter had cleaned dorm rooms at the university in exchange for room and board.)

But when the Hendersons' bumper crop of 1931 was brought in, there was no one to

Despite the wheat surplus that glutted the market and crashed prices, farmers decided to plow up even more land with bigger and bigger equipment.

buy it. Theirs was just one small part of a huge wheat harvest of 250 million bushels, which created a nationwide glut. Grain elevators overflowed, and giant dunes of wheat were stacked out on the open ground. By August, only 40 percent of the crop had found a market. Prices had already collapsed to 25 cents a bushel or lower, roughly half of what it cost the farmer to grow it. "Bewilderment, distraction, despair, would come nearer to suggesting the common state of mind as people are forced into selling their most important means of livelihood for less than the cost of production," Caroline wrote. "We are too big to cry about it, and it hurts us too much to laugh." But the Hendersons, she noted, were at least free of debt on their land and machinery: "We shall, I think, keep on some way. But what of the people who are paying rent, who are in debt for legitimate expenses, who have the expense of illness or larger families to provide for and educate?"

Harry Forester was one of those people: heavily in debt and with nine children to support and educate. But like so many of his neighbors, he could not believe this situation would last for long. They were "next year" people. Things were sure to improve. Like everyone else, that fall Forester went back to the fields and plowed up more land. The same thing was happening up and down the Great Plains—in North and South Dakota, in eastern Montana, Wyoming, Colorado, and New Mexico, in western Nebraska, Kansas, and Oklahoma, and in northern Texas. The response to rock-bottom prices was the same as the response to the sky-high prices that had ignited the Great Plow Up in the first place: plant more crops. By the end of 1931, more than 30 million acres of the southern Plains—an area bigger than the entire state of Ohio—had been stripped of its native sod.

"It was a recipe for economic disaster," according to Donald Worster, because farmers were planting more wheat when an oversupply already existed. And it was a recipe for environmental disaster, because

By the end of 1931, the Kansas "wheat queen" Ida Watkins (above) had quadrupled her acreage in wheat, and Wayne Lewis (on tractor, opposite, left) had helped his father break out more land in Oklahoma. The result was 30 million acres of exposed soil (opposite, above) in a region known for two things: constant winds and fickle weather.

"the basic fundamental fact of the Great Plains is that the only thing that prevents wind erosion is grass. . . . It has evolved to hold that soil in place. If a drought comes along they are lying there vulnerable with so much land that has been exposed."

Pamela Riney-Kehrberg, a historian of the southern Plains, agreed. "There's never been a moment before when they had this group of conditions and this much land potentially available to blow," she said. "In the 1890s, when there were very difficult conditions, there was a lot of grass still out there. Most people in that area were grazing cattle. This [would be] the first big drought after most of the land had been plowed for wheat."

Wayne Lewis didn't need a historian to explain what had been happening and the danger it posed. He was there. Lewis was sixteen years old by the end of 1931, growing up on a 1,000-acre wheat farm with his Quaker family in Beaver County, on the eastern end of the Oklahoma Panhandle. Looking back, it all seemed very clear to him:

We made so much money at raising wheat in the late twenties that we broke everything out to raise more *wheat. And then the climate changed and the Depression came along and the wheat wasn't worth much. But we still had the land broken out.*

We were just too selfish and we were trying to get rich quick off of the wheat. And it didn't work out. That was the lesson of the Dust Bowl.

Chapter 2

MIDNIGHT WITH NO STARS

Through this most lonely and disheartening of winters, I have found my greatest inspiration and encouragement in the blossoming plants in our windows. . . .

Insignificant little things these are, I realize; yet they have seemed to reassure me that sunshine and rain, the laws of life and growth, seedtime and harvest, are in a general way dependable; that our earthly heritage is still rich in possibilities; and that most of our troubles are caused by human faults and follies, and are therefore capable of correction.

—*Caroline Henderson*

DURING THE FIRST TWO YEARS of the 1930s, other parts of the nation had been suffering from serious drought: first the Midwest and the South, along the Ohio and Mississippi river valleys (Arkansas was the hardest hit), then the northern stretches of the West, from the Dakotas through Montana and Idaho to Oregon. To the people on the southern Plains, it all seemed far away—troubles just as distant as the Depression tales of big-city miseries. "These were people that really believed that they could control the environment," said historian R. Douglas Hurt, "or at least that the environment was benign. And they were simply making use of it and would for as long as anyone could project into the future. They really didn't know the environmental history of the Great Plains. But they were soon to find out."

A little after noontime on January 21, 1932, a dust cloud appeared outside of Amarillo, Texas. Dust storms weren't uncommon in the area, but this one rose 10,000 feet into the air and carried winds of 60 miles per hour. It moved across the Panhandle before dissipating. The local weather bureau didn't know what to make of it—calling it "awe-inspiring" and "most spectacular." Even old-timers said they'd never seen anything like it in their lives.

Robert "Boots" McCoy was five years old. His family lived 6 miles west of the Hendersons and about 30 miles east of Boise City. Boots's father, a cattle trader originally from Arkansas, was out on the land, checking on his herd, when Boots and his older sister, Ruby Pauline, saw the big cloud approaching. They both huddled with their mother, who was pregnant at the time. "Scared us to death," he said, nearly eighty years later:

We didn't know what to think. It started way off and it was real, real dark, and the closer it got, it got brown. And it'd be still. Be just as calm as it could be. And then when that dust got there, wham! It would hit you. It was just a rollin'.

And you know, when it hit, in thirty minutes it's just like midnight. Middle of day was just like midnight with no stars. Just dark. You couldn't see your hand in front of your face. And it just choked you and choked you with the dust, it was so fine.

It scared the heck out of us. Mother'd pray about it, you know. And us kids, of course we were little, and we stayed pretty close to Ma, I guarantee you.

The storm passed quickly, but that winter of 1931–32 was uncommonly dry. So was the spring that followed. The

When a "black blizzard" rolled in across the Plains, like this one approaching Springfield, Colorado (above and preceding pages), young Boots McCoy (left) and his sister Ruby Pauline ran to the arms of their mother for reassurance.

fierce winds common to the season began picking up sand and soil from the bare fields and moving it across the landscape. In southwestern Kansas, Lorene Delay White was playing in the yard outside the family's chicken coop-turned-house with her brother and two sisters when clouds appeared on the northwestern horizon. At first she thought they were thunderheads, but something about them didn't seem right. "I didn't know what was coming," she recalled. "I knew that it was something we hadn't had before. So we went in and told Mom and Dad and they came out and looked. And then I thought it was probably a tornado. So I asked them if a tornado was coming. And they said 'No, this is not a tornado.' But it got darker and darker, and I was really afraid. Before it hit us, rabbits ran ahead of it, birds flew ahead of it. And we had never seen anything like it. Maybe the

grown-ups weren't afraid, but I was. You wondered, 'How far was it gonna go? How... where would it stop? Would the house go too?' And then it finally rolled in on us. You couldn't see anything. I remember Mom lit the lamp. It was dark enough that we had to have the lamp."

As the summer wore on, so did the drought. The temperatures kept rising, sometimes topping 110 degrees. And the winds—a constant part of Plains life—now carried a menacing message. "I hated the sound of it," Lorene said. "That was one thing that bothered me: to hear the wind. Once in a while Mom and Dad would leave us at home and I would constantly watch the sky. I was always on watch for a roller to come in. I felt like it was my responsibility to watch after the kids, to take care of them." Try as she might, she could never shake the underlying fear of what might happen next.

Storms came in different types and even colors. A dark roller bears down on a house near Dalhart, Texas (above), while an abrasive sandstorm peppers everything and everyone in its path near Guymon, Oklahoma (left). In Prowers County, Colorado, an expansive brown cloud churns across the flat expanse, picking up more dirt with every mile (opposite, right).

When Lorene Delay White was left in charge of her younger sisters and little brother Dee (above) in south-western Kansas, she worried that the next storm might bury them all. The chicken coop in the background was their home for a while.

For reassurance and strength, she relied on her father, "the strong person in my life. He gave me courage when I would become scared or frightened. Dad only would have to tell me it would be all right and I knew it was. Even if it sounded kind of far-out, I believed what he said. Dad always would tell us, 'It'll be okay. It'll be gone,' and I believed him. He gave us the security we really needed during those dirt storms."

With the dusters becoming more frequent, the weather bureau began classifying them by their type and severity. Some storms, taking the coarser, sandier soils, moved along the ground for a few miles before disappearing. Others created a light haze in the sky. The worst ones reduced visibility to a quarter mile or less. No Man's Land had fourteen of those in 1932. (The Kansas Academy of Science had a more complicated system, with three classes of storms—"rectilinear," "rotational," and "ebullitional"—and seven species within each class, ranging from a "sand-blow" to "funnel storms.")

In the midst of it all, Boots McCoy's mother went into labor. It turned out she was carrying twins. She named them Roy and Troy, but they were in trouble from the very beginning. "They lasted, about best I could remember, about twelve hours," McCoy said. "And when we buried 'em the neighbors built a coffin. And one of them went to the J. C. Penney store and got some size 12 shoe boxes, and we put in some cotton, and put them boys in that and put them in the coffin. That's the way they were buried in '32."

With the summer came the time to harvest the winter wheat. It was a double disaster. Prices had plummeted even lower than the previous year, and, with half the normal moisture, there wasn't much of a crop anyway. "There is hardly one stalk where three or four grew last year," Caroline Henderson reported:

Many fields will not be cut at all. Judging by any standards that the world would recognize, we should have been further ahead if we could have spent the year in sleep.

In nothing that we can produce here is there at present the slightest chance of any return on our labor. Yet we keep on working—really harder than ever. . . .

People still toil amazingly and make a conscious effort to keep cheerful. But it seems to me that the effort grows more apparent. Behind the characteristic American nonchalance one detects a growing anxiety, especially about the coming winter.

Midnight with No Stars **45**

In the fall, farmers went back to the fields and planted winter wheat for the next year. "You kept thinking that tomorrow things will change, so you kept doing what you were doing," Clarence Beck said of his father's and other area farmers' attitude. "Plant over and over again, hoping that this thing was over and you were going to have a crop. They couldn't live without hoping that things were going to change for the better."

"We learn slowly," said Wayne Lewis, "and what didn't work, you tried it harder the next time. You didn't try something different; you just tried it harder, the same thing that didn't work. We always had hope that next year was gonna be better—and even this year was gonna be better."

Caroline Henderson was both practical and philosophical about the situation. "We cannot afford expensive mistakes, and are trying to proceed cautiously," she wrote, adding, "I often think of Christina Rossetti's little poem, 'Uphill,' and begin to realize its truth: 'Does the road wind uphill all the way? Yes, to the very end. Will the day's journey take the whole long day? From morn to night, my friend.' "

Meanwhile, the economic Depression gripping the nation had deepened. One out of every four American wage earners was now out of work. And one out of every four American farmers had lost his land, his home, and his livestock. In Boston, children with cardboard soles in their shoes walked to school past silent shoe factories with padlocked doors. In New York, a jobless couple moved into a cave in Central Park and stayed for a year; they could find nowhere else to live. That year, the National Children's Bureau estimated that a quarter of a million Americans under the age of twenty-one were homeless. Officials of just one of the nation's railroads, the Southern Pacific, reported that 683,000 transients had been discovered moving from town to town in the company's boxcars.

The southern Plains had lost its seeming immunity to the financial catastrophe. In 1931, Haskell County, Kansas, had needed to spend only $3.57 on help for its poor; by the end of 1932, the combination of increased needs and sinking tax revenues (residents couldn't pay their property taxes) put the county on the verge of bankruptcy.

Even holding playful kittens, Will and Caroline Henderson (below, left) look grimly determined as hard times hit the Panhandle. Meanwhile, when the owner of The Coffee Shoppe in Boise City became worried about rumors that his business was folding, he took out an angry ad in *The Boise City News* (below).

Hazel Lucas Shaw (above, with her students at the Plainview School) was among the Cimarron County schoolteachers paid in scrip—IOUs the school district issued in place of checks. When the Boise City Bank (right) refused to cash them, she went on teaching without pay.

School districts issued scrip—paper IOUs—instead of money to its teachers. One Kansas county decided it could reduce its budget by no longer trying to enforce Prohibition laws. In Oklahoma, Cimarron County's sheriff continued to raid country side stills making illegal alcohol, but he often left the confiscated sacks of sugar on the steps of the courthouse in Boise City for anyone to take. Sometimes, he left "roadkill" there, too, for families desperate for food.

Caroline and Will Henderson were hanging on. A real estate bond supposedly worth $1,000—"our only intangible possession"—had been declared worthless, she wrote, but "by sacrificing the small reserves we had held against the days of drought and disaster, we have succeeded so far in keeping on a cash basis":

> We have disconnected the telephone, our only insurance in case of accident or emergency; stopped the daily paper; . . . made hand towels out of the cement sacks which are no longer returnable; substituted cheap lye for washing powder, so that my hands are rough and uncomfortable from week to week. . . .
>
> Many cherished plans have failed. Not only radio and telephone, but running water in the house, furnace heat, modern lighting and refrigeration, have all passed beyond our dreaming. Even the three-cent postage is a burden. . . .
>
> The road ahead seems blocked. All sense of security for our old age has vanished. But we have not given up. We have managed to stay out of debt. We can still eat home-ground wheat cereal. The spring pullets are beginning to lay and the fall calves to arrive. We plan to gather driftwood from the distant river and "cow chips" from our pasture to help out on the winter's fuel supply.
>
> But of all our losses . . . the most distressing is the loss of our self-respect. How can we feel that our work has any dignity or importance when the world places so low a value on the products of our toil?

The Hendersons' neighbor, Harry Forester, had more than his self-respect to worry about. His crop had withered in the drought, and what little wheat he had managed to harvest brought in only 17 cents a bushel. The land he had purchased near Boise City turned out to have a prior claim on its title and was taken from him. The job he relied on, managing the dairy herd for a local state college, was given to someone else with political connections. The mortgage on his original homestead, which he had used to buy the extra land, could not be paid and he lost it, too. "The drought and the Depression came along and just wiped him out," said one of his daughters, Shirley Forester McKenzie, "and so he was scrambling again."

He was forced to move his wife and nine children to rented land. Harry Forester's dream of amassing enough property to give each of his five sons 640 acres was in shambles; now he would struggle simply to keep his large family fed and warm through the winter. "I went out one time and took Dad's lunch out to him or a bucket of water or something to him," Louise Forester Briggs, another daughter, said, "and he stopped the horses and he always knelt down and gave thanks for his food. That just always impressed me that he never failed to do that. And it stuck in my mind. He never let it touch his faith."

THROUGHOUT THE UNITED STATES, things were getting worse. In just one day, one quarter of the entire state of Mississippi went under the auctioneer's hammer. From San Francisco to New York, thousands

The overwhelming vote for Franklin D. Roosevelt in 1932 (right) was an expression of both anger and hope, but the dust storms only got worse in 1933. One of them caught women in Ulysses, Kansas (left and above), out in the open.

of Americans were reduced to living in shantytowns called "Hoovervilles," after the president they had come to blame for everything.

In November 1932, voters took out their despair and anger on Herbert Hoover and elected Franklin Delano Roosevelt to lead the nation through the crisis. Even the normally Republican counties of the southern Plains went Democratic. Roosevelt, they hoped, would at least try to help them. But even a president couldn't control the weather.

In March 1933, when Roosevelt was inaugurated, there was no rain at all in Cimarron County. The agricultural agent predicted that, at best, farmers might harvest 4 bushels of winter wheat per acre, versus previous yields of nearly 30. More than 40 percent of the county's landowners were in arrears for their property taxes.

And now the dust storms were more frequent: instead of the fourteen storms of 1932 classified as the worst, there were thirty-eight in 1933. One storm in April lasted twenty-four hours. In May, another storm forced the celebrity aviator Charles Lindbergh and his wife, flying from Kansas City to Albuquerque, to make an emergency landing on the border of the Texas and Oklahoma Panhandles and wait things out for a day before they could continue. Not only were the storms becoming more prevalent, they were getting larger—no longer localized events, but regional in scope.

"You could hardly avoid looking to the west to see if you could see this rim of dust that was rising on the horizon," said Shirley Forester McKenzie. "And you could see that little rim of dust—it was earth-colored—way far away, beginning to rise. And the next day perhaps it would be bigger and then come quicker and higher. And then suddenly you were just engulfed. It was overhead, and you couldn't see the sun. And day after day it would be that way: dark, black, scary."

Midnight with No Stars 49

The storms came from different directions, took different forms. Some people claimed they could tell where the dirt came from by its color—yellow from Kansas, red from Texas, brown from Oklahoma, and so forth. Others considered the low, hard-driving sandstorms as bad as the towering dirt storms. "It would sting," said Virginia Kerns Frantz, who was growing up in an extended family of a dozen people, living in her grandfather's three-room sod house in Beaver County. "It was just like knives cutting into you when the wind and the sand blew. It just sliced into you." Imogene Davison Glover remembered how the blowing sand tore at her bare legs when she was sent out to get the chickens indoors whenever a sandstorm kicked up.

"It was just unbelievable," said Pauline Heimann Robertson, recalling the difficulty getting from one place to another in Union County, New Mexico. "It'd blister your face. It would put your eyes out. And it would peck the glass on the front of the car and nearly ruin your headlights. It would practically sand off the front of your car. It made enough noise that you couldn't hear very well on the inside of the car, it was hitting the sides of the car that bad. At times it would pick up gravel—not just dust, but gravel. And that's what would take the paint off of your car." Floyd Coen thought the abrasiveness of the blowing sand did more damage to the land and livestock than the dirt storms. "And they might last two or three days," he added. "One time my mother marked twenty-one days on the calendar that we had sandstorms every day."

But nothing was as terrifying as the "black blizzards"—huge, boiling walls of

In Dalhart, Texas, two people watch a storm's approach within a safe distance from their front door.

A Kansas storm boils across the plains (top) and a farmwife (above) tries to get her dog inside before it hits.

fine dirt that rose thousands of feet in the air and sometimes extended more than a hundred miles across the flat horizon. Some people compared them to mountains of loose soil that rose in the distance and then marched across the landscape. Wayne Lewis said it looked like "a tornado that was on its side."

"They were fearful," Floyd Coen said. "You didn't know what was back there, this giant wall just rolling toward you and a lot of turbulence in it. As far as you could see there was a dust storm coming right toward you. And you still had the feeling, whether you would admit it, that something was going to run over you and just crush you. And I think the animals felt the same way. Chickens would go to roost and the horses would run and make a noise and the cattle would run. It was pretty fearful."

Virginia Kerns Frantz would be transfixed watching a storm approach. "It was rolling around and there were different shapes," she said. "As a child, I imagined dragons coming out of it, because they were so scary looking."

Children weren't the only ones whose imaginations saw more than airborne dirt in the black blizzards. Dorothy Christenson Williamson was already in her twenties when the dust storms became a frequent part of life in southeastern Colorado. "There's nowhere you can run," she said. "You can try to get out of it, but it's as if it follows you, follows you, follows you. You can't escape it. It was almost surreal, the dust. You think about a flood or a hurricane, a tornado; you hear about those things. But this dust was something that at least in our country we had never encountered before. And I think it carried with it a feeling of, I don't know the word exactly, of almost being . . ." and she paused in her memory to find just the right word, "evil."

Whenever possible, people hunkered down in their homes for the storm to blow over. Even then, the dust found them, somehow filtering in through cracks in the walls, the crevices in windowsills, the gaps between doors and their frames.

Dorothy Sturdivan Kleffman remembered a particularly bad duster that rolled in during midday at her family's wheat farm a little east of the Hendersons: "And so we all gathered in the kitchen, the whole family. And we lit the kerosene lamp and that didn't help very much. And mother had tea towels that were made out of flour sacks because we were also in the Great Depression at the same time. They were probably about three-by-three-foot squares. And she dipped those in water and we put 'em over our heads and we sat there with these over our heads because we couldn't breathe it was so thick, the dirt. We just draped them over our head, down the face, you know, the whole head. You couldn't see anything. You sat there and you couldn't talk or visit with anybody very much. But that wet towel would catch the dust. And sometimes those towels were pretty black by the time we took 'em off."

Motorists soon learned to either stop their cars and stay put inside them during a storm, or to inch ahead slowly, wary of ending up in a ditch. In December 1933, Caroline and Will Henderson were driving to Texhoma, Oklahoma, 26 miles away, to arrange for tractor repairs, when they got caught in a storm. "They were turning on lights in all the stores by 1:30," she wrote. "We left town about 2:00 and had to creep along burning our lights all the way home. Often we could hardly see the length of the car ahead of us through the clouds of pulverized soil."

Sometimes, the dust and sand moving through the air created static electricity that seemed to surround everything. A car moving through it (unless it was dragging a chain to act as a ground) picked up the charge, "and the more dust and the longer the ride, the higher the charge," said Clarence Beck, "until finally it gets such a powerful charge that if you reached out to touch a car, the electricity would jump out about six inches to meet you and knock you right flat on your butt."

As kids, Dale and Floyd Coen loved sneaking up behind other children and

touching their ear after a storm, making them jump from the shock, or daring each other to see who would extend a hand toward a wire on their farm's windmill that seemed to snap back at them like a spark plug. "I can remember feeling it in my hair," said Dorothy Sturdivan Kleffman. "It was just kind of like your head tingles. Your hair gets kind of wiry. It was a funny feeling. It didn't hurt you. It just felt like your hair just didn't want to stay in place." For Wayne Lewis, the most vivid memory of static electricity was what he saw, not felt: the barbed wire points on the fence row—and occasionally the horns of the cattle—glowed in the night.

After the big wind had gone, that dust would just settle, settle, settle. It'd be so quiet. Oh, ungodly quiet, you know. You could hear birds chirpin' the next morning.

—Robert "Boots" McCoy

There was just dust everyplace. You were living in a dust cloud. But it wasn't always like that. Don't forget, this is a storm, which means it'd have a beginning and an end. And in between storms, it couldn't have been more beautiful. The skies were crystal blue and the clouds were those puffy white summertime clouds— without a drop of water in fifty of 'em.

I can still remember my father looking up at the sky and praying that it'd rain. But naturally it never would. Those weren't rain clouds and never would be.

—Clarence Beck

IN THE TIMES BETWEEN STORMS, when the skies cleared and the winds abated, the farmers and townspeople tried to carry on with their lives. But the land they called home was being rearranged before their very eyes.

"Oh, just dirt, piles of dirt," said Imogene Davison Glover. "If we had something like a plow or anything out in the yard, it might be nearly covered up with dirt; anything that would stop it was banked. And the house had dirt on the south side like two feet deep maybe. But it had all blown away over on the west side and the north side and clear down to the foundation. Anything loose blew away or banked up around something."

The barn at Dorothy Sturdivan Kleffman's farm had a drift so high on one side of it "you could walk up on the roof of the barn . . . like you had a ladder there, but it would be dirt." The barn at Boots McCoy's place had an open face on one side, which "kind of made a vacuum," he said, "and it would suck that sand in. It filled that barn nearly to the rafters." Some farmers, facing the same situation, found it easier to tear their barn down and salvage the wood—or simply burn the barn—than to try to dig out the huge drifts.

The storms had pushed dried-up Russian thistles—tumbleweeds—across the open ground by the hundreds of thousands. Wherever they piled up against barbed wire fences, they created eddies in the wind, and the dust accumulated around the tumbleweeds. "Then the dirt got higher and higher," Virginia Kerns Frantz said, "and it was not uncommon to be able to walk over the top of a fence. You just walked up the side of the drift, walked over the fence, and down on the other side." Boots McCoy remembered riding his horse over the drifted fences to try to find cattle that had already wandered off over the same fences. "So everyplace there'd been a fence was a elongated hill, the height of a fence," according to Clarence Beck. "And if cattle started walking over the fence as they would be able to, the farmer would put a new fence on top of that. So there'd be some places where the land would be surrounded by a dike, two fence posts high."

Over in Union County, New Mexico, Pauline Heimann Robertson remembered the challenge of driving from one place to another on backcountry roads:

There were sand dunes everywhere you went. And the sand would make dunes across the road here, and maybe tomorrow the dune was over there. However the wind hit that sand, it would change the location.

And when we drove, you just wound around and through those sand dunes because you couldn't stay on the road. Sometimes it would cover the road until you couldn't go through with a car. The sand was taller than the car.

Where the dirt and sand hadn't piled up, the land had often been swept clean of topsoil to the depth of a one-way plow. "It was bare, it was hard hard just like cement," said Dorothy Sturdivan Kleffman. "You could take a broom and sweep it just like you could a wood floor." "You could walk out onto your farm and instead of fine dirt, you found this hardpan layer on the top," according to historian Donald Worster. "Impossible to cultivate. Your dirt would be in somebody else's farm or a county away." Virginia Kerns Frantz said, "All the dirt was either piled close by, or else on down into Texas or Colorado or somewhere else where it blew to."

The farmers did their best to break up the hardpan and replant what they could. Meanwhile, their children found a source of fun and treasure in many of the scoured fields. Artifacts that had once been well buried under the topsoil were now in the open—pioneer wagon wheels, branding irons from the cowboy days, Spanish stirrups from the time of the conquistadores, and thousands of Native American arrowheads. Boots McCoy could fill a one-pound coffee can with arrowheads and trade it for candy or a soft drink at the country store. "That ground would be just smooth, but there'd be little wrinkles where a 1-way had gone," he said. "The rest of that topsoil blew away. And the arrowheads would just be lying on top. You could pick 'em up everywhere. I picked up a gold watch and I traded that gold watch for a Nehi grape pop. And my uncle, he busted my boo-hind and told me anytime I found something like that to let him look at it first."

Clarence Beck remembered something else about the new look on the land. "The pigpen is normally thought of as this dirty place," he said, but after one of the big blows, "it got so clean that my sister used it as a playhouse. The sand in there was bright, clean, shiny. And the wood was sandblasted. You couldn't find a nicer, cleaner place to play than the pigpen."

The farm animals themselves, however, were in as much trouble as the land and crops. Chickens that hadn't been gathered into their coops before a big storm hit blew away in the fierce winds. "The livestock that were trapped out in these conditions were

The fierce winds of the dust storms scoured the powder-like dirt from some fields and then dumped it in big dunes in other places, rearranging the landscape.

As more Russian thistles—tumble-weeds—blowing across the land caught on barbed wire fences (above), they formed eddies in the wind where the dirt would deposit, until entire fencerows slowly became sand dunes (right).

devastated," Donald Worster said. "They had no protection whatever. Their lungs filled up with this dirt. They died of suffocation. Birds died of suffocation. Whatever wildlife was out there died of suffocation. But animals also simply wandered away, not knowing where they belonged, and would climb over these dust drifts and be lost. So it was far more devastating for livestock than for humans in terms of loss of life."

Simply making it through a storm didn't mean a cow's survival was secure. The scouring winds damaged farmers' feed crops as well as the wheat. Drifts of dirt smothered the grasses on many parts of the uncultivated rangeland, and forage that wasn't ruined by the dirt and sand wasted away from the desiccating heat and drought. "If the cows ate weeds, which they did sometimes, then we couldn't use the milk," Dorothy Sturdivan Kleffman said. "It tasted terrible. I can't describe it, but I'll always remember the taste of it."

Most homesteads had wells and a windmill near their house, so the families and animals were not entirely without water. Well water could also be used for household gardens, but the abrasive winds, the shifting dirt—even, sometimes, the charge of static electricity in the air—often killed the vegetables families were counting on. "A storm would come and there would be absolutely nothing left of it," Virginia Kerns Frantz said of their family garden. "The wind would cut it off. And mother tried her best to keep that from happening. She would put gunnysacks on the fence to cut down the wind some. She would dig postholes to plant tomatoes in so the wind wouldn't reach them and cut them off and they could get bigger and stronger. And she dug deep rows to put anything in. But of course sometimes they would fill up with dirt."

As if the wind and dust weren't enough, hordes of jackrabbits driven by hunger began swarming over what pastures, crops, and gardens were left. "Nine rabbits would eat as much as a two-year-old steer," Dale Coen said, describing them as the farmers and ranchers saw them: competition for the cattle's dwindling feed. "And the rabbits were so thick that they were just eating everything in sight."

"They ate everything green there was," Dorothy Sturdivan Kleffman said. "The farmers had killed off the coyotes and that upset the natural order of things, and the rabbits just exploded and they would eat anything green they found. They would eat your garden up." Boots McCoy remembered rabbits descending on their farm by the thousands, with appetites that extended beyond green. "They'd eat anything," he said. "Dad put new posts up on our place, and it was cedar post with bark on it. They ate the bark off."

To combat the invasion, entire communities began organizing "rabbit drives." Clarence Beck described them as "a gala event, somewhat similar to a box lunch auction at a country school. You'd advertise it with flyers all over the place in advance: 'On Saturday afternoon on the farm of Joe Smith would be a rabbit drive. Please come. Bring the family.' So on that afternoon, there might be fifty to a hundred families show up. Those families would be dispersed around the perimeter of a square mile of land, like advancing infantry in a battle attack. Every member of the crowd would have a baseball bat or club of some sort."

At a given signal, the circle would begin to close, with everyone making as much noise as possible, driving whatever jackrabbits there were within the perimeter toward the center, where a pen with an open gate waited. "And what started out as a peaceful picnic sort of turned into a riot," according to Beck. "Dogs barking and yipping, people yelling and kids screaming, and rabbits hopping in the air." With the rabbits herded into the pen, the gate was closed. Then some of the men—and often the young boys—climbed in and began killing the animals with their clubs and bats. "We'd kill 'em until we just gave out," Boots McCoy said. "And then more kids would get in and go fightin' 'em. They'd kill 'em by the thousands."

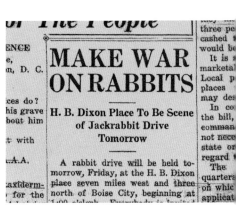

Depending on the condition of the dead rabbits, some were taken home to be skinned and boiled for food, but more likely to feed to hogs; most of them were shipped east by the trainload. The point of the drives was eliminating animals seen as pests. What happened to the carcasses was secondary. One rabbit drive in the Texas Panhandle, where guns were allowed (an "ammo truck for anyone who runs short" was promised in its promotion), killed 6,000 jackrabbits in one afternoon. In Oklahoma, under a headline, "Make War on Rabbits," Boise City's newspaper announced that H. B. Dixon was inviting everyone to his place 13 miles northwest of town, but "Mr. Dixon said due to the danger involved when guns are used, some have requested that two separate drives be held. The drive tomorrow will be for those using clubs. Arrangements for the date of the shotgun drive will be made after the drive tomorrow evening."

Three-quarters of a century later, among the children who lived through those years, memories of the occasional rabbit drives were as vivid as of the ubiquitous dust storms. Besides the general mayhem of the community event, what they all remembered most particularly was a singular sound. "They would scream," Dale Coen said. "And I can still hear rabbits, the noise that they'd make. I went on one rabbit drive and that was enough for me."

Despite the disruptions of the storms, on weekdays children were still expected to attend classes. And the teachers were still expected to be there, even if getting paid for it wasn't guaranteed. After one year of college, in 1931 Ina K Roberts Labrier had begun teaching in one-room country schoolhouses in southeastern Colorado. (Like President Harry S Truman, Ina K's middle name is a letter, without a period.) Her salary of $75 a month was expected to help her parents keep farming. By happenstance, she withdrew $20 from her account the day before the local bank went under, and "we lived on that for weeks," she said. As the Depression deepened, the county went broke as well, and although her paychecks would arrive, she said, "they would just tell us to hold it until they had the money. But sometimes we had to wait four, five months to cash them. Even when I married I think

To combat an explosion in the rabbit population, communities like Boise City promoted rabbit drives (left), which became part social event and part raucous melee. Some drives allowed guns, but most used clubs (below) to kill the rabbits that had been stampeded into a pen.

WESTERN KANSAS RABBIT DRIVE

I had four checks yet that hadn't been paid in eight years."

Besides the normal educational duties, teachers like Labrier now had the extra task of dealing with the dust storms and their aftermath. She often had to drive her students home if a duster struck near the end of the day. "You couldn't tell whether you were on the road or on the sides or where you were," she said, and sometimes she had to stay overnight with a student's family if driving became impossible. "At the time the teachers were also hired as janitors," according to Virginia Kerns Frantz. "That was part of their contract, that they do the janitorial work. And most of them did it very well. But we had one teacher who absolutely refused. He said, 'I see no point in doing that every day when it has to be done again the next day.' So every day we would have dirt that was piled a little bit higher. I think probably at one time it got between two and three inches high. And every day we had to clean the dirt off our desks. You didn't have paper towels available like you do now, or rags. Rags were at a premium too. So you just wiped the desk off, and as a result you had chapped arms. But that's the way you got through to where you could put your paper down—at least to where you could write on it."

Imogene Davison Glover attended a two-story school, near the Henderson homestead in Texas County, that had a big stairway to the second floor. The teacher believed the safest place for her students in a threatening storm was away from the windows and under the stairs. "And I

Students in a one-room Oklahoma school try to concentrate on two things: their studies and keeping their mouths covered against the pervasive dust.

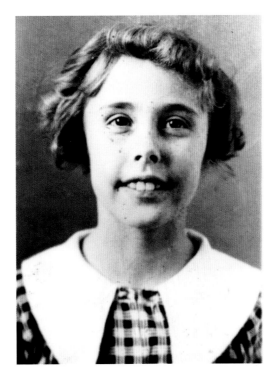

Little Trixie Travis Brown (left) found the brown skies and dirty air depressing and claustrophobic; Dorothy Sturdivan Kleffman (far right) got caught in a dust storm between school and home.

remember when it got worse, the teacher told us to sit down and put our head on our knees, put our arms around our legs, and if the storm knocked the building down, we'd be safe in the stairwell," she said.

Down in Follett, Texas, a constant haze of dirt filled Trixie Travis Brown's school. "I remember the lights were on in our classroom in the middle of the day because it was dreary and dark. And I could look out the window and the atmosphere was just beige. You couldn't see a blue sky. I remember looking out and thinking, 'How depressing.' I was just maybe eight years old or nine years old, and I felt depressed and I felt as if I couldn't breathe. So I told my teacher, 'I can't breathe.' And she said, 'Well you need to go home.' So she called my mother. And of course Mom didn't have a car. I walked home. Mother put me to bed. There was just a little bit of dust on the pillow. We just got used to the smell of dust. It was everywhere."

Not everyone got home from school so safely. One day, Dorothy Sturdivan Kleffman and her brother were headed for home, a mile's walk across pastureland, when she spotted a dust cloud rising in the north: "But I thought, 'I think I can beat that home.' And I got about halfway home and it hit. It was dense enough that I became disoriented, and I wasn't sure whether I was going in the right direction anymore. When it rolled in, it picked up bits of gravel and it hit your bare face and legs and arms and it hurt. It hurt. Then I looked behind me and I saw these car lights coming across the pasture. When he got close enough that his headlights could shine on me, I stepped out into the light, and it was my uncle who had come to school to pick me up but had found out that I had already started home. I don't remember being afraid. I just was going to cope with it as best I could. I never got caught in a storm again after that one. I learned, you know."

Over in Colorado, Calvin Crabill rode a horse to his school, 3 miles from home. Just after his tenth birthday, while he was in fifth grade, he and his schoolmates were outside for recess:

And we looked to the west and there's this black cloud, very low, close to the horizon, a black cloud from left to right as

Teachers always kept their eyes on the horizon for another storm (opposite, top) that could suddenly turn day to night and endanger their students (above). Ina K Labrier (back row, opposite, with her class) made sure each of her students made it home safely. Though he sometimes pretended to be an Indian, Calvin Crabill (opposite, bottom left) was actually a young cowboy, who headed to his herd instead of home when an approaching black blizzard closed his school.

far as the eye could see. As we kept playing, this cloud kept growing. It was black.

And we were frightened. The teacher was frightened. She said, "Children, go home now! Go home now!"

Well I couldn't go home because my job after school was to go round up the stock on the open range. I went to round up the stock. And meanwhile the storm was coming on slowly. It didn't come fast, it came slowly.

The stray cattle were spread over several square miles, and it took Crabill some time to round them all up. Still a good distance from home, he reached a lane that pointed toward the barnyard, got off his horse, and began leading it on foot, worried it would panic because of the approaching storm: "And it hit. And all hell broke loose. It was as loud as any hurricane or thunderstorm you want, but then suddenly it was all dust. All dust. And I was frightened as a little kid. I was just ten years old." Unable to see, he kept moving, feeling his way along the fence line, the herd in front of him.

Meanwhile, when Calvin hadn't showed up at home, his father had set out to search for him in the fierce storm, and was groping up the lane in the other direction. Through the blinding dust, he saw his cattle herd emerge. Then the riderless horse. "When he first saw the horse with no rider, he thought maybe I'd been thrown off or something," Crabill said. "He was very frightened. But then he saw me. Well, he hugged me. He was so worried. He expected me to get home myself when the storm approached and ignore the animals. But I didn't because that was my duty at the time. I brought the stock in."

Chapter 3

THE CRUCIBLE

I remember one time it rained and we were all just thrilled. The children went out in the streets, barefoot and dancing in the rain. We let the rain fall on our tongues, and we were just ecstatic. When our mothers called that it was time to come in for supper, nobody would go in.

So finally the neighbors all brought supper to the front porches and we had supper on the front porches and more dancing in the streets. It was wonderful. We thought maybe the tide had turned. But you know, after that here came the dust again.

—Pauline Durrett Robertson

IN THE EARLY SPRING OF 1934, a snowstorm blanketed No Man's Land. The flakes, mixed with airborne dirt, were darkened. A "snuster," not a duster, the locals called it. But at least it was a little moisture. In the Texas Panhandle, a light rain fell. Many people thought the drought had broken. "The goose hangs high," a local newspaper reported. "[Farmers are] going down the furrow with brighter days in sight and a song in their hearts." Soon enough, they realized how terribly wrong they had been.

A nationwide drought now affected forty-six of the forty-eight states (all but Maine and Vermont), and 1934 would turn out to be even drier than the years before. In May, the temperature had already reached 100 degrees in North Dakota, where the drought was a year older. Parts of Nebraska, where temperatures hit 118, were already blowing.

On May 9, a massive weather front moving eastward began picking up loose soil from barren fields in Wyoming and Montana, then Nebraska and the Dakotas. Ultimately, 350 million tons of dust were lifted tens of thousands of feet in the air. Carried by high-level winds, the gigantic cloud crossed Iowa, Minnesota, and Wisconsin, and as it passed over Chicago, it deposited an estimated 12 million pounds of dust—4 pounds for each resident of the city.

On May 10, it darkened the skies over Detroit, Cleveland, and Buffalo. By the morning of May 11, the storm enveloped the eastern seaboard, from Boston to Savannah, Georgia. Lingering snowbanks in New England turned brown. A fresh coat of floor wax at the state police headquarters in Westchester County, New York, was ruined by the thick dust.

In New York City, streetlights were turned on at midday. The thick haze obscured tourists' views of Central Park from the top of the Empire State Building, and a ship delayed its entry into the harbor because the captain had trouble seeing the Statue of Liberty to help him navigate. In Washington, D.C., dust descended on the National Mall, even sifted into the White House, where President Roosevelt was holding a press conference promising relief to the drought-stricken Great Plains. The next day, ships 300 miles out into the Atlantic Ocean reported dirt falling onto their decks.

Shocked Easterners didn't know what to think of it. Though it originated on the northern Plains, they referred to it all as "Kansas dust." And many of them quickly had ideas about how to stop it from blowing across the continent. A Chicago business believed covering the Plains with its waterproof paper might do the job, while a steel company in Pittsburgh thought its wire

ONE OF SOUTH DAKOTA'S "BLACK BLIZZARDS" 1934

The huge dust storm of May 9, 1934, began in the Dakotas (top) but dropped dirt all the way across the eastern half of the country and 300 miles out into the Atlantic; by May 11, even the newspaper in Gastonia, North Carolina, was alarmed.

Preceding pages:
A father and son in Cimarron County, Oklahoma, survey the damage to their farm by a dust storm.

netting would work better. The Barber Asphalt Company of New Jersey estimated it could spread an "asphalt emulsion" over the land for $5 an acre. A woman from North Carolina suggested that shipping junk autos west would simultaneously beautify her state while stopping the wind erosion on the Plains.

Other ideas included building wind deflectors 250 feet high, or planting Jerusalem artichokes, or using rocks from the Rocky Mountains, or spreading leaves and garbage from eastern cities. Someone else proposed using concrete, with holes carefully placed for planting seeds. None of the suggestions seemed to take into consideration that the area in question was 100 million acres.

President Roosevelt and his administration had ideas of their own—from encouraging farmers and ranchers to plant fewer crops and raise fewer livestock to finding ways to stabilize the loose soils

through better farming techniques—but those programs were still in their infancy. Whether they would work was anyone's guess. During a stop in drought-ravaged North Dakota on his way to the Pacific Northwest that summer, Roosevelt admitted as much. "I would not try to fool you by saying we know the solution" to the crisis, he said. "We don't. What I can tell you from the bottom of my heart . . . is this: If it is possible for us to solve the problem, we are going to do it."

Some of the people lining the route of his motorcade held up signs that noted how Roosevelt had already ended Prohibition. YOU GAVE US BEER, the placards said, NOW GIVE US WATER. Roosevelt acknowledged their message, and responded, "That beer part was easy."

A series of rains fell shortly after the president's visit and helped ease the drought on the northern Plains. People there called it "Roosevelt weather." But farther south,

there was no such relief. While the outlines of the worst-hit area would shift over the years, sometimes broadening or narrowing, by the summer of 1934, the government had officially identified the geographic heart of the dust crisis. It was near Boise City in Cimarron County, the western tip of Oklahoma: in No Man's Land. One-third of the county's land was blowing. Even pastures of native buffalo grass that had not been plowed had been buried under drifts of dirt, some 10 feet high.

The new Agricultural Adjustment Administration (AAA), created in the flurry of Roosevelt's "First Hundred Days" to address the nation's agricultural crisis, had begun making payments to farmers who reduced their production of wheat (and corn, cotton, rice, and tobacco). In Cimarron County, more than a thousand wheat farmers had already signed up. And other New Deal programs—aimed at easing the effects of the national Depression—had now reached the southern Plains. In 1934, needy Cimarron County residents received 2 tons of smoked pork, 16 tons of beef, 17

tons of flour, and 33 tons of coal through a surplus commodities program. Twelve hundred people—a quarter of the county's population—depended to some extent on New Deal jobs.

But that did not address the other calamity, which compounded the misery of the Great Depression. "We are getting deeper and deeper in dust," the *Boise City News* reported. The same was true in all the other surrounding counties in Texas, New Mexico, Colorado, Kansas, and the Oklahoma Panhandle. Only a little more than two years into the drought "the environmental catastrophe on the Great Plains was pretty clear," according to Donald Worster. "It would have at that point classified as one of the worst environmental disasters in American history already."

Caught in the crucible of dust, drought, and Depression, the battered residents of the area around No Man's Land weren't thinking in historical terms. They were focused on surviving the moment, though always trying to look toward "next year."

"We are trying to hope that for all this

During his tour of the dust-ravaged Plains in 1934, President Roosevelt was greeted by signs like this one, reminding him that ending Prohibition didn't satisfy the land's thirst: "You Gave Us Beer, Now Give Us Water."

The Annual Gamble

A farmer near Boise City examines the damage to his land (right), while a cartoon in the *Boise City News* (above) illustrates "the annual gamble" facing him in 1934.

drought-stricken area, which includes parts of five states centering around our Panhandle county, the worst is over," a weary Caroline Henderson wrote her Easterner friend. "Yet today, after we thought the drought had been effectively broken and the windstorms had ceased, we had another terrible day of violent wind, drifting clouds of dust, and Russian thistles racing like mad across the plains and piling up in head-high impassable banks and barricades at every fencerow or other obstruction."

She and Will had signed a contract with the AAA to reduce their wheat plantings by 39 acres and were eagerly awaiting their government check. "I suppose," she wrote, "they will get around sometime and ought to be a great help, not only to the farmers but to the businessmen in all the little towns which depend exclusively on farm trade. . . . We feel as if the administration is really making a sincere effort to improve general conditions, but they have a tremendous task, made harder of course

by all who cling tenaciously to special privileges or opportunities of the past."

By fall, conditions on the parched rangeland had deteriorated so badly, the tumbleweeds Caroline Henderson had described as "racing like mad" across the land and piling up at fencerows had shifted from nuisance to food source. "By saving two big stacks of Russian thistles, which seem to be able to grow without rain, and every bit of feed that grew," she wrote, "we hope to be able to get our herd of cattle through the winter, as they are worthless on the market at present." Cimarron County officially declared "Russian Thistle Week" and dispatched relief workers to help ranchers harvest them for fodder.

In nearby Union County, New Mexico, young Pauline Heimann Robertson and her brother were put to work helping make the weeds more palatable: "Daddy said 'We don't have enough money to buy food for the cattle, but if we can cut thistles and stack 'em, there's more food value in that than nearly anything.' And our job was to

tramp those thistles down. Now if you want a bad job, that's one. Those thistles would get down your pant legs into your shoes, those little stickers, and you can stand it about so long, but pretty soon you've got to stop to get out a sticker. But that's what we did." Some ranchers had even ground up yucca cactus or burned off the spines of prickly pears in an effort to give their cattle something to eat. The way things were going, a worried agricultural agent said, "The coming winter is going to test the mettle of the Oklahoma people."

Roosevelt's administration announced a new federal program, designed primarily to stabilize beef prices by reducing the nation-wide surplus of cattle, but in the drought area it also meant to deal with the problem of cattle wasting away for lack of adequate pasturage. In Cimarron County, farmers and ranchers were invited to the Palace Theater in Boise City to hear the details. To encourage them to cull their herds, the government would pay them up to $16 a head for any cow healthy enough to be

shipped to a packing house, where it would be slaughtered and canned for distribution to families on relief. Cattle deemed unfit for consumption would bring a minimum of $1 a head, but these would have to be immediately killed and buried.

As a natural grassland, the southern Plains had once teemed with bison, which had been eliminated to make way for cattle. Now, with so much of the grassland plowed up for wheat and blowing in the wind, it was the cattle's turn. Government agents fanned out across No Man's Land to make the purchases, oversee the shipments, and where necessary pay men for putting their herds under the drifting soil. Desperate as they were for some income, it was a bitter pill for many of the stockmen to swallow. Harder still on their children.

"It was the most traumatic thing as a little kid I'd ever seen," Calvin Crabill remembered. "What they did was they took a bulldozer and made a mammoth ditch and drove all the cattle down in there. And then there were men above with rifles—I

Horses and cattle (top) on a farm next to Dorothy Sturdivan Kleffman's scrounge for fodder on the desic-cated land; some cows became so emaciated that the government paid farmers $1 a head to shoot them (above) and bury the carcasses.

would say maybe ten or twenty men with rifles—and they shot the cattle. I'll never forget to my dying day standing there as a little boy when they started shooting those cattle. It's a sight that the average person couldn't stand, but as a little kid it was very rough 'cause that was our stock. You got some money for it, but that didn't matter. They killed the stock."

Seventy-five years after the fact, Pauline Heimann Robertson broke into tears recalling similar events at her father's ranch:

The government came in with this program and they said that we're going to have to do something with those cattle because we can't let 'em all starve to death. So daddy said, 'I'm interested. What do you have in mind?'

And they said, 'Well, we can come in here with big equipment and we can dig a ditch, and if you can get cowboys to get those cattle together we'll just rush 'em and they'll fall in that ditch and then we'll kill 'em and cover 'em up.'

And daddy could hardly do that. I never will forget my brother and me standing there and watching them shoot those little calves. They killed all those cows and they killed those calves. My estimate was about two hundred head.

In Cimarron County, the government purchased 12,499 head of cattle in 1934, paying $164,449 to local ranchers. Nearly 20 percent of the cattle were deemed too frail to be shipped (versus less than 3 percent in the state of Kansas) and had to be shot. Some needy families in Boise City were allowed to attend the cattle kills and cart off the meat, if it was not diseased. Nationwide, $111 million was spent to purchase 8.3 million cattle. A similar program did the same thing with hogs. The oversupply of livestock had been eliminated, and prices began to rise. That year alone, on this and other programs dealing with the drought crisis, the United States spent half as much as it had spent to fight World War I.

Cattle deemed healthy enough for slaughter were shipped to stock-yards and their meat was distributed to the needy; farmers got $16 for each cow.

The Dust Bowl was a double whammy. They suffered from the Depression just like everybody else did. But when the dust started, almost every day was just made miserable for existence. And they couldn't get their lives back together until the drought was over.

So they weathered two disasters instead of one.

—*Trixie Travis Brown*

BY 1934, PROPERTY VALUES around Boise City had declined by 90 percent, and more than half of the landowners were delinquent on their taxes. Each week, the local paper carried notices of upcoming sheriff's sales of farms being put on the auction block because of unpaid mortgages. In 1929, during the Great Plow Up, local farmers had also borrowed a million dollars to buy new equipment. In the five years since then, they were able to repay only a quarter of it.

Every farm, every business was affected. The telephone company that had opened in the rural part of No Man's Land went under, because so many of its customers, like Caroline Henderson, had stopped service to save money. The Palace Theater shut its doors—until enough people persuaded the owner to reopen, on the promise

they would gladly pay 10 cents to watch movies that helped them take their mind off their troubles. No one knew what the next calamity would be or when the hard times might end.

"The pressures on husbands and fathers were significant because after all they were responsible in the traditional way of thinking about things to care for their families, to provide an income," said historian Pamela Riney-Kehrberg, who studied the social impact of the Dust Bowl. "And here they were in a situation where the land simply wasn't allowing you to do that. The way husbands and fathers adapted as they watched their fields blow was to simply try, try again. It could be extremely difficult and extremely stressful. And the tension in a lot of households was palpable."

When he lost yet another crop to the drought, Pauline Arnett Hodges's father found himself hard up against his mortgage. His farm was half paid for. "I think he must have been scared to death because he had relatively little education," she said. "Farming was all he knew how to do, all he'd ever done. And to look out and see in that field solid mounds of dust. He'd say, 'Oh Dora, it's going to get better. It'll get better.' And he would talk about his banker in Liberal and he'd say, 'Mr. Igo is going to

The new house that Trixie Travis Brown's family had bought in Follett, Texas, during the boom years was repossessed by the bank when her father's hardware store went bankrupt.

Pauline Arnett Hodges was six years old (above) when the bank foreclosed on the family farm in Beaver County, Oklahoma; her father, she said, was never the same afterward. Trixie Travis Brown's grandparents (above, right, with family members) also lost everything to the "double whammy" of drought and Depression.

let us continue for a little while longer. If we just had a crop we could pay off that mortgage.' Finally, the bank was desperate, and in the winter of 1934–35 they foreclosed. And of course we lost our farm."

They moved into a vacant three-room house in town, a place without electricity or running water that rented for $5 a month. Her father took up drinking. "I think my father not only lost the farm but he lost all hope he had of things ever getting any better," Pauline said. He finally managed to find a government job building roads that helped keep the family fed, making $3 a day, then $5 when he was promoted to foreman. "But even as young as I was," she said, "I remember seeing the change in him, from the self-confident person that he'd been to somebody who was really defeated. And frankly he never recovered. I think now, looking back, that he was humiliated because he'd had such high hopes. Maybe the only saving grace was there were a lot of people around us also losing their farms."

On the main street of Follett, Texas, Trixie Travis Brown's father and grandfather were trying to hold on to the hardware business they had opened a few years earlier. Among those having trouble paying their bills were a pair of brothers, valued

customers and friends, she said: "The two of them came in to the hardware store and talked to Grandpa and said, 'I don't know what we're going to do. We're wiped out. We cannot pay this bill that we owe you right now.' Grandpa could see how desperate they were, and he said, 'Don't worry about it. We'll carry this. You'll be just fine. We'll get our money.' And it was no time before the tragedy happened. One of them—he had a family with children who were in school with me—hanged himself at home. And the other one also did, but someone was able to find him before he was dead."

Soon enough, neither her grandfather nor her father could carry the debts they had incurred in their business. The hardware store went bankrupt, and as part of the proceeding the bank took the family's house. "Mom and Dad did not really explain to us why we were moving," Trixie said. "I was confused. I couldn't understand why we were moving out of a nice house into a dilapidated house. But my parents did not discuss finances in front of us. Never did." Her grandfather lived on a ranch where he only had $600 of debt. But, she said, he "lost his cattle, he lost his section of land, he lost his home, and he lost his health." Only in his late fifties, he

When Millard Fowler (far left) went to ask for permission to marry his girlfriend, Esther (left), he found his future father-in-law in the midst of attempting suicide because of a series of financial reverses.

and his wife moved into Follett's downtown, where Trixie's grandmother opened a small sewing shop and he spent his days, suffering from asthma and unable to work, sitting in front of the shopwindow, talking with anyone who passed by. "This," Trixie said, "was the sort of agony going on."

In Bazine, Kansas, a doctor took his own life. "He told us just a few days ago that money was an impossibility now," the local paper reported, "and the letters indicate that financial troubles are the cause of his act." A thirteen-year-old Dodge City boy, said to be worried that his parents couldn't afford his schoolbooks, committed suicide. Devastated by his investment losses, a Cimarron County doctor killed his wife and then himself.

In Boise City, Millard Fowler was fresh out of high school and ready to build a future. He had fallen in love with the daughter of one of the area's prominent families. "They had grain elevators and a wholesale oil business and a car agency," he said. "You know, the things that just absolutely went really broke. And they lost everything." Fowler and his sweetheart decided to get married, but first he wanted to get her father's blessing. Fowler found his future father-in-law sitting in his car in front of the family home:

When I opened the door I didn't know what he was up to. But I saw that rifle pointin' at his head. I got in the seat beside him, and took that rifle and unloaded it without any conversation as I remember.

But I finally got around and asked him if it would be all right if we got married, and he finally said yes. A couple of months later he committed suicide.

Fowler and his fiancée went on with the wedding, but because of the tragedy and the hard times, it was a modest affair. "When we got married I had to go across the street to get the barber to come over to witness. And that was our wedding party," he said. "I had an aunt that gave us a dozen old hens. Her sister gave us another dozen. And we moved out on a ranch south of Boise City, in a little cowboy shack about ten by twenty I think, a little one-room cardboard shack. And we brought those chickens down there and made a pen for 'em. And that way we always had something to eat. If you've got chickens you can eat the eggs and then when they quit layin' you can eat the chickens. But we finally ate 'em all up—either that or the coyotes got 'em,

Shaw Funeral Home
EFFICIENT AND HELPFUL SERVICE
CHARLES C. SHAW
Funeral Director

Boise City Phone 167   Keyes Phone 13

Hazel Lucas and Charles Shaw (top), both schoolteachers in No Man's Land, had married and started trying to have a family after Charles studied to be a mortician and opened a funeral home in Boise City (above); then the hard times hit.

cause we finally ran out of chickens. And we moved back to town then. We had a pretty slow start."

[Sometimes] we stood spellbound at the sight of the wide expanse of prairie land, stretching for miles in any direction that we chose to look! . . . [T]he beauty of the wide-open spaces where we had spent most of our lives struck us with a force . . . for this [was] our homeland.

—*Hazel Lucas Shaw*

BY THE SPRING OF 1934, Hazel Lucas Shaw was thirty years old and had been living in No Man's Land for twenty of them—ever since her father took out a homestead south of Boise City during the wheat boom of 1914 and then moved his family to it by covered wagon. She had grown up loving the sweeping vistas of the southern Plains and looked forward to

To reach his expectant wife at the closest hospital, 45 miles from Boise City, Charles Shaw had to drive through a black blizzard like the one above; he made it just before Hazel gave birth to their daughter, Ruth Nell (left).

making a career and then starting her own family in the same place.

Hazel was determined to be a teacher. By age seventeen she had her certificate and was working in the rural schools of Cimarron County. By age eighteen she had met and married another teacher, Charles Shaw, who went into the mortuary business, running the funeral home in Boise City, just across the street from the Methodist Church. Even when the school district paid her in scrip that turned out to be worthless, Hazel kept on working for a couple of years, but by 1934 she had left her job. For more than a decade, the Shaws had been hoping for children. By early April she was expecting—and had been waiting for a week at the hospital in Clayton, New Mexico, for her baby to arrive.

Charles was at work in Boise City on April 7 when he got the call that the big moment was near. The hospital was 45 miles away on unpaved roads. A dust storm was brewing as he headed out in his Model T. "The roads had drifted pretty much full, in big drifts of dirt just like snowdrifts across the road," said their son, also named Charles. "He started out and he got stuck in one of the drifts. And so he jumped out of the car, and went on a couple of miles to a farmer's house. They got the tractor, came back, and by the time that they got back, the dirt had all blown away from the car."

Farther on, at a turn in the road, the car swerved into the ditch and flipped over. Bruised but not badly injured, Shaw managed somehow to get the car upright—and made it to the hospital just as Hazel entered her final contractions. They named their daughter Ruth Nell, and for several weeks the new parents lived with anxiety about the baby's health, which required a number of trips from Boise City to Clayton to consult with doctors. But "suddenly," Hazel wrote, "Ruth Nell became plump and happy, a beautiful child, who was the joy of our lives and the pet of all who knew her."

Later that year, the Shaws were reminded of how lucky they were. One bitterly cold winter day, while caring for Ruth Nell, Hazel looked across the street and saw a cardboard coffee box on the steps of the Methodist Church, covered by a coat. Before she could go over to investigate, the minister came out, removed the coat, and discovered a little baby in the box. He rushed it over to the Shaw house, where they tended to the newborn and called the doctor and police.

"And that little baby was just about four pounds or such," Charles Shaw said. "It wasn't very large at all. It became known in the community as the 'coffee box baby.' And Mom said that a lot of people wanted to adopt it. It had been left there by some unknown person, some mother that couldn't take care of it in those particular days, I guess. It was adopted by a couple there in town and it first seemed to thrive. But within a year it passed away."

As 1934 ended, the people of the southern Plains could look back on one of the driest and hottest years on record. Rainfall in a number of communities had measured less than 10 inches. Dodge City, Kansas, had suffered more than fifty days with temperatures over 100 degrees. No one wanted to dwell on the past. They preferred to look forward—to "next year," 1935.

But the Plains, historian Walter Prescott Webb once wrote, comprise a "semidesert with a desert heart." Given the combination of the drought and the farming practices of the day, fellow historian R. Douglas Hurt said, "unless there was a substantial rainfall, there was really not much in sight except more of the same. People really thought that things probably couldn't get worse. But it got worse."

Chapter 4

DUST TO EAT

I can shut my eyes and feel yet the rush of an almost painful thankfulness when we looked out over our fields [in the 1920s] and watched our ripening grain bending, rising, bending again in golden waves swept interminably by the restless wind. It seemed as if at last our dreams were coming true.

. . . Yet now our daily physical torture, confusion of mind, gradual wearing down of courage, seem to make that long continued hope look like a vanishing dream.

There are days when for hours at a time we cannot see the windmill fifty feet from the kitchen door. There are days when for briefer periods one cannot distinguish the windows from the solid wall because of the solid blackness of the raging storm.

Only in some Inferno-like dream could anyone visualize the terrifying lurid red light when portions of Texas are "on the air."

—*Caroline Henderson*

IN 1935, CAROLINE HENDERSON and her neighbors would learn that the driest, hottest years, like 1934, were followed by the biggest, fiercest dust storms. The area around No Man's Land would be subjected to twice as many storms of the worst category as the year before. And most of them struck in the first four months.

During that time, seven different storms reduced visibility to zero in Amarillo, Texas. One single storm destroyed a quarter of the wheat crop in Oklahoma, half of the Kansas crop, and all of Nebraska's. It blew out 5 million acres of fields, and in the space of a day carried off twice as much dirt as had been excavated by the United States in the decade it took to dig the Panama Canal.

During a black blizzard in February, a farmer's car went off the road 2 miles from his home, and he got out to walk the rest of the way. He never made it. In March, a seven-year-old boy near Hays, Kansas, got caught alone in a storm. Searchers found him the next morning, dead from suffocation, smothered in dirt. Farther west, a nine-year-old wandered off alone in the same storm; when he was discovered, he was tangled in barbed wire, but still breathing. Eastern Colorado reported six deaths caused by dust storms in a two-week period.

Rural schools closed for weeks at a time because of the dust; in Alva, Oklahoma, a college basketball game was cancelled because the gymnasium air was permeated with dirt. The train from Kansas City to

Residents of Guymon, Oklahoma (above), just south of Caroline Henderson's homestead, prepare for another storm's assault.

Preceding pages:
A farmer leans into the blowing dust on what had been his cropland.

A paperboy in Ness City, Kansas, needed goggles and a dust mask to make his rounds (above), and shop-keepers in Syracuse, Kansas, used both brooms and shovels to clean their sidewalks (right).

Dalhart, Texas, was forced to stop when its passengers complained they were choking; it paused long enough to let the dust settle, while people scooped out the dirt on the floors and seats.

In Garden City, Kansas, the local hardware store sold out of the goggles people wore to keep dirt out of their eyes; then the train delivering a new supply was delayed—by a dust storm. A geologist in the state measured the suspended particles in a sample of the air over Wichita and estimated 167 tons of dust per square mile. During the month of April, southwestern Kansas would report only five dust-free days and the windiest month on record. Writing from Great Bend, where an uncorked jug became half-filled with dirt in two hours, a journalist wrote: "Lady Godiva could ride through the streets without even the horse seeing her."

Tucumcari, New Mexico, suffered $288,000 in property damages in just one month. Merchants in Amarillo estimated that the ubiquitous dust had reduced the value of their merchandise by 3 to 15 percent.

After surveying the residents of Meade, Kansas, a reporter calculated that the average for a single storm was $25 worth of damage per home, $10 per automobile, or $7.20 per person. What couldn't be measured, the reporter said, was "the loss of disposition of the housewives."

"This was a terribly difficult time to be a mother, to be a homemaker, to be trying to keep a nice house for your family," according to social historian Pamela Riney-Kehrberg. "Every time you turned around there's more dirt in the air, there's more mess to clean up. It's as if the whole world is falling in on you. You could be completely crushed by this situation. It was very, very fine dust, blown by the wind, and it would get into any structure. It got into poorly built farm homes; it also got into nicely built houses in town. There was no way to get away from this dust."

Imogene Davison Glover's mother, like so many other housewives, tried everything she could think of to keep the dust at bay. "I can remember mother having us tear up old rags into strips about two inches wide

and we'd stuff them in the cracks around the windows and the doors and then we'd make paste out of flour and water and sealed up everything that we could," she said. "But it was still terrible. You scooped out the dirt— you didn't sweep it out, you scooped it out. Mother would finally get it cleaned out, but the next day we'd have another dust storm."

At the Forester home, not far away, the older girls were expected to help with the cleaning, according to Shirley Forester McKenzie:

My sister and I, on a clear day, on a Saturday morning, would start at the top floor and take a broom—we didn't have a vacuum in those days—and sweep the dirt off of the windowsill, and then take the curtains down, take them out and shake them and leave them out a while.

And it was so thick on the dresser, we'd sweep it off. And then we'd get a shovel and scoop the dirt into a washtub—a big washtub—and carry it out. Then we'd go start again and go from the top and go down, and get a much smaller amount the second time.

And then *we'd take dustcloths and wipe the furniture off.*

Trixie Travis Brown recalled a neighbor's wife who normally prided herself on the cleanliness of her house: "Her husband brought one of his business associates in and they were making some plans about where to move the cattle. They were at the dining room table and they weren't using pencil and paper. They were writing in the dust on the table. And she was humiliated." To take advantage of the "least dusty days," Trixie's own mother would wash the family's clothes ("our washing machines were the rotating old tub type; we had no dryers of course") and hang them out to dry, only to have them "come in dirty; it was terribly discouraging."

"My mother was very clean," Dorothy Sturdivan Kleffman said. "Her house was always clean and she tried to keep us kids clean. She would take all her curtains down one day and wash them and hang them back up. A dirt storm would come in that night, and they would be just like they were before she washed them. That went on day after day after day. And once in a while, you would hear of some woman that just couldn't take it anymore and she'd commit suicide."

The Boise City News offered gummed tape to help housewives protect their homes from the invasive dust, but nothing seemed effective, so the indoor battle against dirt (top, right) seemed never-ending. The girls in the Forester family (Marilyn and Louise, top, left, in front of recently cleaned window curtains) learned that each effort between storms usually required two complete dustings.

In Topeka, Kansas, the Red Cross called in scores of seamstresses (above) to make cloth dust masks by the tens of thousands; in Dodge City (right), people wore goggles and masks from World War I.

Living with the dust became part of the daily routine, and since some storms arrived after sundown, it was part of the nighttime routine as well. "Before we went to bed, we covered the water bucket with a cloth so that the dust wouldn't get in the water overnight," Dorothy said. "We went to bed, and when we got up the next morning our covers would be completely covered with dust. The only clean place on our pillow would be where our head had laid. All the rest was covered by dust. My mother would go in the kitchen and before she could do breakfast she had to wipe off all of the cabinets, all of the tables. Everything in there was covered with dust. She had to clean the kitchen before she could even cook breakfast. It came in that bad."

Virtually every family eventually adopted the habit of turning their plates upside down until it was time to eat. Plates left the other way would simply accumulate dirt on the food's side. The same applied to drinking glasses. "You'd turn 'em over and shake 'em, look at 'em before you put anything in them," said Floyd Coen. "My family thinks that I'm kind of stupid, and I guess I am, but I still, if I get a glass out of a cabinet, I rinse it out before I drink out of it."

Over time, the dirt gathered in places not as immediately noticeable. "My sister slept with my parents," Imogene Davison Glover said. "Doretta was probably about a year old. And the ceiling of our house was covered with sheetrock. And it was so full of dirt between the sheetrock and the roof that one night while I was sleeping in the next room I heard Daddy yell, 'Grab that kid, Mom!' And they hit the floor and ran from where that piece of sheetrock was straight above their bed. That sheetrock fell on the bed and it was probably three or four inches deep with dirt."

In Dodge City that year, after two other ceilings collapsed from dirt that had sifted through the roof, a man went into business cleaning attics with a big carpet sweeper, sucking the dust into gallon pails that he then emptied outdoors. He cleaned more than 200 attics and estimated that each one had 2 tons of dust in it. Even years later, when Dorothy Sturdivan Kleffman's husband, an electrician, was hired to rewire some of the older homes, "he couldn't get a wire down in the wall," she said, "because halfway up, they were full of packed dust."

"You never really escaped the dust," said writer Timothy Egan, who interviewed many survivors. "And that's, I think, what drove people crazy. It always found its way in. One woman told me it was like a snake. She could hear it slithering along the ceiling and then along the side of the wall. And so she said she just waited for that snake to strike from anyplace. She knew it was always there."

Dust to eat and dust to breathe and dust to drink. Dust in the beds and in the flour bin, on dishes and walls and windows, in hair and eyes and ears and teeth and throats, to say nothing of the heaped-up accumulation on floors and windowsills after one of the bad days.

This wind-driven dust, fine as the finest flour, penetrates wherever air can go.

—Caroline Henderson

THAT SPRING, A WAVE OF respiratory illnesses swept across the southern Plains, with symptoms of coughing spells and high temperatures, nausea, chest pains, and shortness of breath. Old people and anyone with asthma, bronchitis, or tuberculosis were susceptible, but particularly infants and young children.

Everyone understood why so many of the people they knew were coming down with it. The tiny particles of dust suffusing the air in their homes and yards and farms very easily made their way into people's lungs. "Anytime you took a breath, you had dirt," explained Virginia Kerns Frantz. Imogene Davison Glover compared going through a dust storm, particularly outdoors, in more graphic terms: "If you'd go out and pick up a handful of dirt and stick it in your mouth, that's just the way it would feel. I don't know how to tell you any different. It was just pretty bad."

The prairie dust itself did not carry any infectious bacteria, the Kansas Board of Health determined after an intensive study, but it was high in silicon particles, "as much a body poison as is lead . . . the most widespread and insidious of all hazards in the environment of mankind." Exposure to the dust irritated the mucous membranes of the respiratory system, contributed to other infections, and in time could result in silicosis, a disease more commonly associated with miners who worked underground for all their lives.

Whatever the science behind it all, people called it "dust pneumonia" and considered it a vicious menace. The soil they had turned over during the Great Plow Up had already killed the sodbusters' crops and livestock. Now it seemed to have zeroed in on something much more precious: their children.

Virginia Kerns Frantz came down with it, coughing up what she called "a bunch of gunk. Well, the gunk you coughed up was mud." The nearest doctor was 60 miles away, she said, "so I was doctored with kerosene and lard and turpentine that was rubbed on your chest. And for cough syrup you had sugar with a drop or two of kerosene in it. That was your cough

Two girls in Baca County, Colorado, try to pump water while protecting their mouths in March 1935.

syrup." Dorothy Sturdivan Kleffman's parents brought in a doctor for her little sister; he treated her with a poultice of onions and mustard applied to her chest, "and as a child I thought, 'Well, what good would vegetables do?'" In Boots McCoy's neighborhood, anyone showing symptoms of dust pneumonia was wrapped in warm blankets and given hot toddies made with bootleg whiskey, in hopes they would sweat the disease out. Imogene Davison Glover's mother took her little brother all the way to the hospital in Amarillo, Texas, and worriedly watched over him as he became delirious from fever. "He was pretty sick," Imogene said. "He always had aftereffects. We were just lucky that he lived through it, 'cause a lot of them didn't."

Nervous mothers redoubled their efforts to seal off their homes from the menacing dust clouds (often in vain) and badgered their children, whenever they went outside, to wear a variety of masks the Red Cross had begun distributing. "It

was scary to me as a child because I'd never had anything like that. And it frightened me, at least at first," said Pauline Arnett Hodges. "I got over that and I thought it was uncomfortable and I hated it. But it was better than coughing and choking all the time." Floyd Coen wasn't so sure: "You put it on and there's a certain amount of moisture—I think kids have more moisture in their mouths but you just couldn't get a good breath after it was on awhile because it'd be soaked up from the dirt on the outside. And what I heard more than anything else was, 'Floyd, put your mask back on.' I hated to wear it. I could get a better breath without it than I could with it, I thought."

Not far from the Coens, in the southwestern corner of Kansas, Lorene Delay White's parents insisted she wear strips of sheets over her nose and mouth, but to little effect. The dirt "would get in the air and so you breathed it," she said. "I'm sure Mom and Dad were concerned about what it would do to us, but there were times when it

An entrepreneur in Wakeeney, Kansas, came up with a giant vacuum to suck out the dirt from attics and even from buried lawns.

When Lorene Delay White (far left, at right in the photo) came down with dust pneumonia, her father (left) feared he would never see his daughter again.

was hard to breathe because of the dust. You had more of a suffocating feeling, like you couldn't breathe real well." Lorene was an otherwise healthy teenager when suddenly she started running a high temperature:

> Dad knew that it was probably pneumonia. There was no doctor near us. Dad went to Richfield, which was about seventeen miles from home—they had a drugstore there then—and the druggist gave Dad the only medicine he knew that would help me. And I thought about it later, it was Alka-Seltzer. And I hated taking it.

> But I kept getting worse. It was hard for me to breathe with the dust. So Dad built a frame around my bed and put sheets around my bed. And he wet them down. And then I couldn't breathe, because I couldn't get any air in there. I was having a hard time breathing anyway, and that only made it worse.

Lorene's parents decided her only hope was to move her to relatives farther east, away from the ever-present dust. Her mother would go with her, but her father needed to stay and try to manage the farm. "The day they came to get me, the dust was terrible," Lorene said. "We weren't having a roller storm but a dust storm that was awful. You could hardly see to drive." With her temperature raging, she was far too weak to walk, so her father wrapped her in a blanket and carried her to the car.

That's all she could remember of that day. She couldn't remember being put in the automobile, or the four-hour car ride to her aunt and uncle's house, or being taken from the car to their bedroom, or what happened for several more days. And only later did her father, the pillar of strength in her life, tell her what he was thinking when he carried her to the waiting car: "He thought he would never see me alive again."

"I have six children," she added, "and I can't imagine what it would be like to be in a situation like that. He couldn't go with me. He had to send me, and him stay. As a parent I wonder how people stood it, how they endured it. I wonder how Dad kept his courage—and there were lots more like Dad."

At her relatives' home, Lorene's temperature eventually went down, but her coughing wouldn't stop. At night, her mother would sometimes come into the room, "and she laid down on my bed and just sobbed." One day Lorene looked up from where she was lying and saw something through a crack in the door. It was her father. "No words can tell you how tickled I was to see my dad," she said. "And when he saw me and saw how I was coughing, he knew that they had to take me to the hospital." They moved her farther east, to a hospital in Great Bend, Kansas, where doctors finally saved her with an operation that drained the fluid that had collected in her inflamed lungs.

By now, the Red Cross had declared a medical emergency in the area around No Man's Land. Makeshift hospital wards were opened wherever space could be found: the basements of two churches in Guymon, Oklahoma; the high school in Baca County, Colorado, where the senior class play was cancelled because cots now covered the gym floor; even a former sanitarium that had once been a fresh-air retreat for tuberculosis sufferers now hung wet sheets across its windows to protect the patients brought in for dust pneumonia. More than half of all admissions to hospitals in southwestern Kansas were now for dust-related breathing ailments. The Red Cross issued a call for 10,000 more masks. It wasn't nearly enough. More people got sick.

By that spring of 1935, Edgar and Rena Coen had eight children. Six years earlier, Edgar had started work on a big home for his family so they could finally move out of their dugout. But because of the Depression, construction had ended at the basement. They covered it with a sheet iron roof and moved in. It was larger than the dugout—space for two bedrooms and a large room that served as a combined kitchen, dining room, and living room— but it was still underground.

In 1932, twins had arrived: Ralph and Rena Marie, their only daughter, who quickly became the family favorite. "She was just the sweetest little thing you ever saw," Floyd Coen said. "She was just a joy for all of us." His brother Dale explained, "Rena Marie was our only sister. And she was so precious to us because the folks had been trying for a girl all the time, but it always came out boys. She was frail, but she was a pretty little girl." With a family that large, all the older boys had specific duties to help their mother. One of Dale's jobs was to watch over Rena Marie.

"When I came home from school, I'd take care of the twins while my momma was getting supper," he said. "Of the evening, they were beginning to get tired, and they needed quite a bit of help. So Momma kind of insisted on having one of us staying there. And so it fell to my lot—I didn't necessarily volunteer but I didn't mind doing it. But of a night, since Momma had a lot of work to do with seven boys and washing on the board and stuff, she needed a rest. So Rena Marie would sleep close to me. Richard slept close to little Ralph. So I spent an awful lot of time with her."

That spring, four of the Coen children got sick: Floyd, Richard, and the two-and-a-half-year-old twins. One night, Rena Marie's temperature skyrocketed. "We were sitting at the table eating," Dale remembered, "and she just immediately was bathed in water. Water was running off her face and head." She was moved to the bed in the parents' room.

The doctor was sent for and ushered in to see her. Dale was out in the big room, sitting near the woodstove, "kind of out of the way." But he could hear everything going on in the parents' bedroom with little Rena Marie: "She was crying, calling for me to come to her. She called for me, not Momma, not Dad, but for Dale." Then the crying stopped.

Floyd was also in the front room, sharing a bed with Richard and little Ralph, the others sick with dust pneumonia. "The hardest part," he remembered, "was when I heard the doctor say, 'Do you have a

Six of the eight Coen children with their grandparents: Floyd is at bottom right, just in front of the family's only girl, Rena Marie, on her grandfather's knee. Dale, at top left, was given the chore of looking after his little sister when his mother was busy with other tasks.

board?' And my dad said, 'Well, we have leaves for the table.' And he took the table leaf in there and put her little body on that leaf, and brought it out and showed us boys before he took her. And then the doctor put her in the rear seat of his car and took her to the mortuary. That was the hardest thing on me. And still is. She was such a perfect little thing."

"It was bad, bad, bad," Dale said. "And I haven't really ever got over it. I didn't cry much till the next day. And then I went out by myself and I cried for a long, long time." Interviewed in their eighties, both men had trouble keeping back tears discussing the event so long ago. Dale brought along a poem his mother had written about the death of her only daughter:

A little pink rose in my garden grew,
The tiniest one of all;
Twas kissed by the sun, caressed by the dew,
Oh little pink rose, 'twas you.

Oh little pink rose of your mother's heart,
Have you faded and gone away?
Has the Gard'ner gathered my little pink rose,
For his loveliest garden today?

Did He need one more blossom of your size and hue?
And was that the reason the Gard'ner chose you?
Oh little pink rose of your mother's heart,
Have you faded and gone away?

Ah, no, not faded and gone away,
As some are prone to say,
But safely laid in the Savior's arms,
And that's where you are today.

Two weeks later, the Coens' first grandchild, Verle's son, Dwayne, died at age five weeks. He and Rena Marie would be 2 of the 31 people who perished from dust pneumonia that spring in Morton County, population 4,092. The town of Liberal lost nine to the illness. In the

Dust pneumonia hit the extended Coen family particularly hard. Two-and-a-half-year-old Rena Marie, the only daughter (opposite left, with her twin brother Ralph), did not survive it. And then five-week-old Dwayne (opposite, bottom) died from the disease, too. The Rolla Cemetery (right) in southwestern Kansas was covered with dirt and sand drifts when the Coens buried their daughter and grandson.

seven southwestern Kansas counties, nearly 1,500 people became sick with it.

A doctor across the border in Guymon, Oklahoma, said he treated 56 patients for it, including a seemingly perfectly fit farmhand. After looking down the seventeen-year-old's throat, the doctor said, "Young man, you are filled with dirt." Three days later, the boy died. (Even as late as the 1980s, doctors in the region said they could tell if a person had lived in the southern Plains during the 1930s by looking at their chest X-rays, according to social historian Pamela Riney-Kehrberg, "because there was a halo of dirt in their lungs even fifty years later.")

As more children died, some parents began to see a larger force at work. Boots McCoy remembered people in Boise City saying they saw the image of Christ in one of the dust storms. "There was just lots of talk that God was tormentin' us because they plowed up that good sod," he said. On its front page, the *Boise City News* published a quotation from the Bible, the book of Ezekiel: "Behold, I have smitten my hand at thy dishonest gain which thou has made, and at thy blood which has been in the midst of thee."

Back in the 1920s, Caroline Henderson had declared herself a Unitarian and withdrawn from the local church over disagreements with its minister's teachings. But she still kept track of what was being said from area pulpits:

> *A revival preacher—a true Job's comforter—proclaims that the drought is a direct punishment for our sins. . . . Some would-be prophets are sure that the days of grace and mercy and rain for this great prairie land are forever past; that the future promises only hopeless and permanent desert conditions. Others, according to their own words, are quite as sure that fervent prayer is the one thing needful to bring relief.*
>
> *Special prayers for rain were offered at our county seat last Sunday morning. The afternoon brought one of the most sudden, dense, and suffocating dust storms of the season.*
>
> *—Caroline Henderson*

Chapter 5

THE END OF THE WORLD

It seemed that the black dust was always with us. If a quiet day happened to be our lot, the time was spent scooping out the sand of the storm of yesterday. It seemed that we lived in a land of haze. The atmosphere seemed to always be closing in around us, creating an eerie and uneasy feeling.

—Hazel Lucas Shaw

IN APRIL 1935, HAZEL LUCAS SHAW's daughter, Ruth Nell, was nearing her first birthday. She was a precocious child, already speaking some words. But now she, too, was sick. Hazel tried everything to keep the dust away from her baby—lubricating Ruth Nell's nostrils with Vaseline, trying to keep a mask over her face, covering her crib. "Mom said she had every crack stuffed with rags and she would wet them down," according to her son, Charles. "She had hung sheets over everything where dust might come in. But it didn't keep it out. It would come in somewhere."

Ruth Nell began to cough incessantly. Hazel decided she needed to be taken away from Boise City and the dirt-filled air of No Man's Land, and on April 5 she went by train with her to Enid, Oklahoma, 270 miles to the east, where relatives could help her care for her baby. But shortly after their arrival, Ruth Nell's temperature shot up to 103 degrees, and Hazel rushed her to the city's hospital. Ruth Nell's fever would not subside. She couldn't keep milk down. She cried and coughed even more.

Hazel called her husband from the hospital to say he should come as quickly as possible. Just as he had the day his daughter was born a year earlier, he jumped in his Model T and left Boise City. And just as before, he soon ran into a dust storm. "He had to drive with his head outside the window because the dirt was caking on the windshield so bad he couldn't see," his son said. Static electricity shorted out his car and brought it to a stop. Shaw had to wait

an hour to get it started again, then moved on slowly, keeping two wheels on the edge of the ditch as the only way to know where the road was. "When he got to Enid, he was just black from head to toe with dirt, and nothing but the white of his eyes were showing," his son said. "And he arrived only minutes before Ruth Nell died. He had a few minutes with her. But she left just soon after that."

That same day, back on the Lucas homestead south of Boise City, Hazel's grandmother, the matriarch of the clan, was also suffering from dust pneumonia—coughing and running a fever. "Grandma Lou" was eighty years old, with forty grandchildren and thirty great-grandchildren. In her final minutes, she asked about little Ruth Nell, then turned her face away and stopped breathing.

The Shaw Funeral Home and hearse (top) in Boise City; Ruth Nell Shaw (above) on her first birthday.

Preceding pages:
The devastating "Black Sunday" storm marches toward Boise City, April 14, 1935.

Despite efforts to keep the tracks clear in Kansas (below, right), trains still got stuck in the drifting sand, like this one in Dodge City (above).

The Shaws decided that a service for the two, the oldest and the youngest of the extended family, would be held in Boise City, in the church across from their funeral home. Grandma Lou would be buried in Texhoma, near her homestead, but Ruth Nell would be taken back to Enid. "The main reason for that was the fact that Enid Cemetery was visible," Charles Shaw said. "They would have buried Ruth Nell in the Boise City cemetery, except you couldn't even find the tombstones, the headstones, in the cemetery, it was so drifted full of dirt. Mom and Dad just did not want to bury Ruth Nell there in all that dust and dirt." The family settled on April 14, 1935, for the double funeral: Palm Sunday, a week before Easter.

On the Wednesday preceding the services, a black blizzard rolled in, notable for both its intensity and duration. In Boise City, merchants closed their shops so they could escort schoolchildren home in the darkness that shrouded the early afternoon. Just to the west, in Baca County, Colorado, where the dust had been blowing for five straight days, local stores ran out of dust masks and other supplies to combat the dirt. Across the border in Kansas, a rain briefly mixed in with the dust storm, and people said that for a while, mud balls were falling from the sky. A train derailed near Great Bend, and the crew sent to its rescue became stranded along the way for two days by the blowing dust. In the Texas Panhandle, rural schools had already closed a month early, because the volunteer board members were not only concerned about the safety of the students, they were tired of

shoveling the dirt out of classrooms every morning. As far away as Austin, members of the Texas Senate donned surgical masks while they conducted business.

By Sunday, when the day of the double funeral arrived for the Shaws, the storm had finally passed. "When they got up that day it was clear," Charles Shaw said. "A pretty day. And if you've got to do a job like that, you know that's a blessing to your heart if you have a nice day for a funeral for a loved one."

The Shaws weren't alone in their feelings that Palm Sunday had brought with it an unexpected blessing. Throughout the area around No Man's Land that morning, as many families prepared for church, residents were being greeted by a glorious break in the weather. "The Sunday itself was so gorgeous and windless," said Timothy Egan, "and people came out of their dugouts and cleaned their sheets and opened up their windows. And it was like a dawn. It was like a new day. And you thought, 'My God, this land can make us whole again. My God, the worst is over.'"

In Texas County, Harry Forester hitched up a team of horses and loaded his large family onto an open wagon. They all headed a mile and a half down the road to hear an itinerant preacher, enjoying the chance to be outside and together. "Meadowlarks were singing; it was just a perfect morning," said Louise Forester Briggs. "And I was so happy we were going to church."

In Follett, Texas, Trixie Travis Brown's mother hung laundry out on the line, flung open the windows of her house to let in the fresh air, and announced that the family would enjoy the rest of the day out in the country. "The sky was blue; there wasn't a breath of wind," Trixie remembered. "We were just exhilarated, the whole family. And we couldn't understand it either because it just was so abnormal. Mother and Dad decided we would take a picnic. They'd pack a picnic with thermoses of iced tea and water. And we went down

on Wolf Creek, where the creek was not running but there were little puddles that we could wade in. Mother and Dad picked wild persimmons to can for jelly later. And we were all having a grand time."

By midday, the temperature had risen into the high 70s under the azure skies. But farther north, a cold front sweeping down from Canada had begun moving across the Great Plains, pushing a wind before it, picking up more and more loose soil with each mile it traveled. Denver, on the front's western edge, was covered by a haze, and temperatures dropped 25 degrees in an hour's time.

A little later, the front reached Union County, in the northeastern corner of New Mexico, where nine-year-old Sam Arguello and his family lived. Sam was playing in the front yard of their home, nestled in a bend of a canyon with 60-foot embankments looming on two sides, when something made him look up:

And there was a big black cloud coming in. And when that thing came over, I ran into the house and I told 'em, I said, "There's a big black cloud coming out there." And everybody said, "There's no clouds out there." It was a beautiful sunny day. By the time they got to the

Trixie Travis Brown (below, at right in photo) and her siblings on a picnic like the one their family took on the morning of April 14, 1935.

After the monster dust storm crossed Baca County, Colorado (top), it swept into Union County, New Mexico, where young Sam Arguello (above) was playing in his family's yard.

door, it was just black. Everything was black. You couldn't see anything.

We sat at the table, a homemade table that my dad had made. And we had two kerosene lamps on the table. We were sitting across from each other, the guests and us. And you could just barely distinguish them, because that dust was solid. It was just thick, it was just solid dirt. Just like being in a cave with dirt coming down on top of you. Everything was dirty.

Everybody was praying; everybody was praying. There were more prayers said that day than there have been in this whole part of the country—since then or before then.

The residents around No Man's Land already had four years of experience with dust storms of all kinds. But to a person, this one seemed different: bigger, blacker, more sinister.

South of Sam Arguello in Union County, Pauline Heimann Robertson's family saw it approach from the north. "I'll never forget," she said. "We saw this cloud coming in, just black, black dirt. We stood there and watched it until the parents said, 'Run for the house!' And we did. I'll never forget my grandmother—she was pretty much Christian—and she said, 'You kids run and get together. The end of the world's comin'.' And boy that was law and gospel, because Grandma said so. And we all got together and we were scared to death. That cloud just rolled, just kept comin', and it just got dark as could be."

By now it was much bigger than the storm earlier in the week, even bigger than

About a block and a half from his home, at the intersection of Stillman Street and Stevens Avenue in Elkhart, Kansas, Ed Stewart managed to take a series of photographs as the storm approached and then overtook his town, eventually enveloping everything into total darkness.

Like the unlucky people in this automobile in the Texas Panhandle, Trixie Travis Brown and her family had to seek shelter in their car when the storm caught them by surprise.

the monstrous black blizzard of 1934. As it moved south and east across the open fields of Kansas, Oklahoma, and Texas, it got bigger still. It was 200 miles wide, with winds up to 65 miles per hour.

And it began catching more and more people out in the open. The skies were still clear in Boise City when the funeral for Grandma Lou Lucas and little Ruth Nell Shaw had finished. Most of the family, with the exception of Charles and Hazel Shaw and a few others, had left in a line of cars toward Texhoma, 40 miles away, for the grandmother's burial. "They got about a little bit more than six miles out of Boise City when the funeral procession saw the black duster behind them," the younger Charles Shaw said. "And so they knew that they had to do something. They knew they weren't gonna make it to Texhoma before the dust storm hit. And they weren't gonna make it back to Boise City, either."

Farther east, the Forester family's church service had also ended while the skies were still blue. In the playground, the children were enjoying the swing and merry-go-round in the clear air, said Louise Forester Briggs:

We were playing and adults standing around talking, and pretty soon, someone noticed a dark, dark line across the horizon to the north. And someone says, "Looks like we're gonna have a norther." And everybody agreed. They kept on talkin' and a few minutes later someone says, "That's sure comin' on fast." And everyone agreed and said, "Well maybe we oughta be headin' home."

So everybody loaded up in their cars and we got in our wagon and started home. By the time we went a half a mile that horrific storm rolled down on us. It was just like a huge rolling pin coming down on you, or a steamroller.

I was petrified. It just was the overwhelming feeling of that big thing rolling down on you, and the wind blowing you practically out of the wagon, when you're a little thing like I was.

A mile from home, Harry Forester realized they could go no farther in the teeth of the storm. He managed to find refuge in a neighbor's house. "I have no idea what time it was, but I'm sure it wasn't bedtime," Louise said, "and I cuddled up next to my mom and went to sleep." For her mother and father, sleep wasn't possible. Their eldest son, Slats, had a job keeping track of the cattle on a huge ranch nearby. That morning, before the family left for church, he had headed out alone on his horse to ride the range.

In the northeastern corner of the Texas Panhandle, Trixie Travis Brown's family was in the midst of their picnic at Wolf Creek, 20 miles from home:

We noticed what looked like rain clouds forming in the north. But they were growing very fast. It was moving differently. Rain clouds have a blue cast to them. There was no blue in this one. It was black, and churning.

We all got into the car very quickly. Dad and Mom wet anything that was in the car—shirts, towels, handkerchiefs—and put them around all of our faces, and we hunkered down in the car with these wet things around our faces.

And when it hit, the car just did a jiggle from side to side. I don't remember any sound from any people. But it was black. It was totally black. It seemed to take an awfully long time to get by. Nobody cried. There were three of us little children in the backseat. Nobody was crying. I'm sure that was because Mother and Dad were able to keep it together.

In Guymon, Oklahoma, the parents of eight-year-old Boots McCoy had dropped him and his big sister, Ruby Pauline, off for Sunday school, promising to pick them up when it was over. Then the storm hit. "They finally stopped the church because it was gettin' so bad," McCoy said. "People were gettin' up and leavin' anyway. And the pastor excused everybody with a prayer."

The April 14 storm, about to engulf the business district of Ulysses, Kansas.

Boots McCoy and his sister, Ruby Pauline (above), were in church in Guymon, Oklahoma, when the storm hit and the pastor stopped the services. At right, the parking lot is nearly empty and one person, barely visible, appears to be fleeing as the huge cloud bears down on the Church of God in Ulysses, Kansas.

At the top of the church steps, Boots stood there, holding the railing with one hand and Ruby Pauline's hand with the other. "She was more scared than I was," he said, "and I was leadin' her down." They could hear people in the street—parents calling for their children:

> We listened to these people hollerin', but you couldn't see 'em. You couldn't see the car; you'd just go to the voice, you know, people comin' out of the church where somebody was to pick 'em up. But we couldn't hear Dad and Mom, and we became afraid they were back home. So I just took sister and we started.

> We didn't go down the street; we went through the alleys and through the neighbors' yards. Ruby Pauline had a little handkerchief, and she was holdin' it over her mouth. And I had one, too, and I was holdin' it over my mouth and nose.

> It was unbelievable. You could just barely see the ground in places; in other places you couldn't see the ground. It was hard to walk. We had to cross the railroad and I put my hand on the rail—you could feel that train for a long

ways—and I couldn't feel nothin' so we went across the railroad track.

Through the darkness, relying on memory more than eyesight, they finally made it home, twenty blocks from the church. But the house was empty. Their parents were frantically searching for them outside the church and along the main streets. Finally, his parents returned:

> And it was so dark in the house that they couldn't see us. And Mom was cryin' and hollerin' that we weren't home. She was wantin' to go back to see if they could find us.

> And we hollered and said we were home. And it relieved 'em quite a lot. Then we all just sat, and Mom just cried.

> We got to hug Mom a lot, you know, to get her to hush.

After the funeral in Boise City, Hazel Lucas Shaw and her husband had not accompanied the caravan of cars headed for Grandma Lou's graveside service. They had stayed behind, not wanting to leave the body of Ruth Nell. Their young

niece, Carol, five years old, had been told to remain with them. But when she saw the storm approaching, Carol scampered home without telling anyone. As soon as the elder Charles Shaw noticed she was gone, "he hoped that she had gotten home," the younger Charles Shaw said. "But when one of those black dusters hit, the static electricity was so terrible that you couldn't make a telephone call. There wasn't such a thing as ringing up your brother and asking if their child had gotten home all right." The only thing to do was go to the house himself. By this time the darkness was so impenetrable, even Shaw's flashlight was no good to him.

"So he got down on his stomach, not on his hands and knees but his stomach, and he elbowed his way," his son said. "Underneath the dust, you could see a little bit. And so he elbowed his way those five blocks to his brother's house. Fortunately Carol was there and she had arrived home safely." But because the phone service was knocked out, there was no way to let Hazel know that Carol was unharmed: "Dad didn't want to worry Mom, so he crawled on his stomach the five blocks back to the funeral home."

Meanwhile, the funeral procession for Grandma Lou that had started for

3:00 P.M.
The Black Blizzard of Sunday, April 14 '35
Stovall Studio - Dodge City. Kansas

Charles and Hazel Lucas Shaw, already grieving from the funeral of their daughter that morning, became alarmed when their niece, Carol (opposite, far left), left their house unannounced just before the storm hit. Charles had to crawl on his belly for five blocks across Boise City (left) to make sure she had arrived at her home safely. A pair of headlights and some store lights, all that was visible at midday in Dodge City (above), show why April 14, 1935, came to be called "Black Sunday."

Texhoma earlier in the day had turned around for Boise City, Charles Shaw said:

> In order to find a road back, there were four men in white shirts that held hands and stretched themselves across the width of the road, and the lead car got right behind them. And each car followed the one in front of it.
>
> But the four men had to walk back to Boise City, feeling for the edge of the road with their feet to see that they didn't drop off in the bar ditch, which was full of soft dirt and they would have gotten stuck.
>
> It took them a number of hours to get back that way, the six or so miles they had to walk. That's as fast as the procession came back. I think they got back about ten o'clock that night.

April 14, 1935, came to be called "Black Sunday," and no one who lived through it would ever forget the storm's size or ferocity, or what they did to survive it.

After huddling in their parked car while the blackness engulfed them, Trixie Travis Brown's family inched their way home. But when they arrived, although the worst of the storm was over, "we couldn't get into the house," she said. "The dust and dirt was so high that we couldn't open the screen door. So Dad had to go to the garage to get a shovel. And he had to shovel the dirt away from the screen door before we could get in." The sight inside was not pretty: "We had left the house open because mother had said, 'We'll air out things.' So the house was totally loaded with dirt."

For Sam Arguello, after sitting in a pitch-black room "for about four hours, I would say, by sundown it had gone past. It was just as red as it could be to the west,

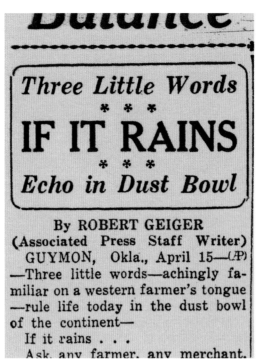

Three Little Words
* * *
IF IT RAINS
* * *
Echo in Dust Bowl

By ROBERT GEIGER
(Associated Press Staff Writer)
GUYMON, Okla., April 15—(Æ)
—Three little words—achingly familiar on a western farmer's tongue
—rule life today in the dust bowl of the continent—
If it rains . . .
Ask any farmer, any merchant.

Slats Forester (far left) was rounding up cattle when the dust storm struck. Robert Geiger's Associated Press story (left) gave the Dust Bowl its name.

where the sun was hittin' it. It was just red all over. My grandmother scared the tar out of me. 'What is that, all that red out there?' I said, 'coming on the west side?' She said, 'It's fire, fire. The world's comin' to an end.' And I went and crawled under the bed."

"It kept on lasting, and it blew and it blew," said Pauline Heimann Robertson, whose own grandmother had already proclaimed the end of the world when the storm first hit. "And I remember when we went to bed thinking, 'Well, the end of the world hadn't happened yet, but what's gonna happen next, you know?' And the next morning it was just dirt on everything. I mean it was black dirt on everything."

Harry Forester had gotten most of his family to safety in a neighbor's house when the Black Sunday storm descended upon them. But he and his wife were worried about Slats, their oldest. Early the next morning, Forester headed for home; everyone else came a little later. "And the chickens were still sitting around with their backs to the north, with their feathers just stuffed with dust," Louise Forester Briggs said. "They couldn't hardly shake it. And so we'd pick 'em up and shake 'em and help 'em get out of it. We kids, that was our job.

And I guess my dad had already tended to the cows and tried to milk them, because they hadn't been milked the night before."

Slats was found asleep in his bed. "He had been caught about three or four miles from home west of us," Louise said. "And he got his horse to follow the fence line, but she got to where she wouldn't walk when she couldn't see. So he got off and had to lead her along the fence line. They got home by suppertime. But he just went to bed like everyone else and covered up his head to forget it."

For Boots McCoy's family, the joy of their reunion in their darkened home was short-lived. Within a month, both Boots and his sister, Ruby Pauline, age eleven, would come down with dust pneumonia. He would suffer lung ailments the rest of his life. She died before summer arrived. "She was my best buddy," he remembered sadly. "We went through some tough times together."

"At least," her mother said after Ruby Pauline was buried, "she won't have to live through another dust storm."

Woody Guthrie (above) was trapped in a house in Pampa, Texas, during Black Sunday—which he commemorated with both songs and drawings (top).

"Black Sunday is the dirt storm that everybody remembered," said historian Pamela Riney-Kehrberg. "It was so much darker, so much more intense, so much scarier than most of the others had been. And I don't think that it's really any coincidence that the outward migration of those who were going to go, came after Black Sunday. People who've been waiting for next year lose hope in there being a next year on the southern Plains after 1935. Not everybody, but those who are inclined to lose hope, definitely lose hope in 1935."

Soon enough, many of the "next year" people would decide to leave the Dust Bowl behind and try to start a new life somewhere else. Among them would be a twenty-two-year-old itinerant songwriter who had found sanctuary from the fury of Black Sunday in a small house with his family and friends in Pampa, Texas, just south of No Man's Land. His name was Woody Guthrie, and he described the event five years later to folklorist Alan Lomax:

BY CHANCE, A REPORTER from the Associated Press named Robert Geiger, along with photographer Harry Eisenhard, had been in No Man's Land on Black Sunday and managed to find shelter in Boise City during the worst of the storm. The story he filed the next day began: "Three little words, achingly familiar on a Western farmer's tongue, rule life today in the dust bowl of the continent—if it rains."

But instead of focusing on those three little words—"if it rains"—more people fastened onto the three words he had used to describe the place that rain had forsaken: "the dust bowl." It was the first time anyone had used that term.

Black Sunday had provided the Dust Bowl with its name. But it also served as a turning point for many of the people within its boundaries. "It caught people unawares," said historian Donald Worster. "They had all become too optimistic again, and they were out doing what people normally do on a Sunday, going to church, doing all those sorts of things. And this storm hits them. And for many of them it was the undoing."

We watched the dust storm come up, like the Red Sea closing in on the Israel children. . . . And I'm telling you it got so black when that thing hit, we all run into the house. . . . We sat there in a little old room, and it got so dark that you couldn't see your hand before your face, you couldn't see anybody in the room. You could turn on an electric lightbulb, a good, strong electric lightbulb in a little room and that electric lightbulb hanging in the room looked just about like a cigarette burning. . . .

And a lot of the people in the crowd that was religious-minded and they was up pretty well on their scriptures, and they said, "Well, boys, girls, friends, and relatives, this is the end. This is the end of the world."

And everybody just said, "Well, so long, it's been good to know you." I made up a little song there—kind of one of my own making. It's called "So Long, It's Been Good to Know You."

Chapter 6

REAPING THE WHIRLWIND

We lived in a brown world. The land was barren and brown. It seemed like most of the houses were weather-beaten. The ground was brown; everything was brown.

There was just not much green. One lady who had moved here from Tennessee, she even watered the thistles because they were the only green thing around. She didn't realize it was a weed.

But in my life it was a brown world. And I didn't know any difference. It was all I knew.

—*Dorothy Sturdivan Kleffman*

BY THE SUMMER OF 1935, many residents of the area that had just been named the Dust Bowl began to worry that they were becoming a forgotten people in a forgotten part of the nation. Like everyone else in the United States, they were suffering as the nation's greatest economic cataclysm, the Great Depression, lingered on. But they were also caught in the midst of the country's biggest ecological catastrophe. And as Black Sunday had so dramatically demonstrated, just when it seemed that things could not get any worse, the drought that added immeasurably to their miseries only deepened, and the dust storms that wreaked such havoc on their lives and spirits only intensified.

At her homestead in No Man's Land, Caroline Henderson sat down and wrote a letter to the Secretary of Agriculture, Henry A. Wallace, to let him know what she, her husband, and so many of her neighbors were going through:

We are [now] facing a fourth year of failure.... Since 1931 the record

Preceding pages:
A solitary girl stands on a sand dune covering her front yard, near Amarillo, Texas.

The small town of Mills, New Mexico, in between storms (below) and in the midst of swirling dust (opposite, left).

Children (above, right) parceling out precious water to a family garden in New Mexico.

has been one of practically unbroken drought, resulting in complete exhaustion of subsoil moisture, the stripping of our fields of all protective covering and the progressive pulverization of the subsurface soil.

There can be no wheat for us in 1935. . . . Native grass pastures are permanently damaged, in many cases hopelessly ruined, smothered under by drifted sand. Fences are buried under banks of thistles and hard packed earth. . . . Less traveled roads are impassable, covered deep under sand or the finer silt-like loam. Orchards, groves, and hedgerows cultivated for many years with patient care are dead or dying. The black locusts which once gave something of grace and distinction to our own little corner are now turned into a small pile of fence posts. . . .

Over much of this area the wind and eroding sand have obliterated even the traces of cultivation. Pastures have changed to barren wastes and dooryards around humble little homes have become scenes of dusty desolation.

In one . . . respect we realize that some farmers have themselves contributed to this reaping of the whirlwind. Under the stimulus of wartime prices and . . . through the use of tractors and improved machinery, large areas of buffalo grass and bluestem pasture lands were broken for wheat raising. [This] has helped to intensify the serious effect of the long drought and violent winds.

During the first half of the 1930s, all but two of the forty-eight states had experienced some form of drought, and farmers everywhere were hurting. But none more than those in the area surrounding Boise City, Oklahoma, which the federal government had declared as the geographic center of the Dust Bowl, where conditions were the worst. In 1935, Boise City received fewer than 10 inches of precipitation, the official definition of a desert.

Farmers in nearby Baca County, Colorado, who had harvested wheat on 237,400 acres of former grassland in the bumper year of 1931, now had successful crops on only 516. In the Texas and Oklahoma Panhandles, the "suitcase farmers," who had hoped to strike it rich with wheat, simply abandoned nearly 4 million acres of exposed fields, leaving them to blow with each new wind. The

weather station in Amarillo counted thirty consecutive days when airborne dirt limited visibility to less than a mile.

In southwestern Kansas, vegetable gardens were producing 90 percent less than normal, and more than a quarter of the children were reported to be at least 10 percent underweight. People "have given up trying to be civilized," a local minister said. "We are merely trying to exist." From Boise City, the commissioners of Cimarron County sent a desperate telegram to Washington, saying: "80 percent of residents in county in dire need of immediate relief to save them from semi-starvation."

For every family, food and nourishment took on starker meaning. In Beaver County, Oklahoma, young Virginia Kerns Frantz, who had survived dust pneumonia, went to check on a calf that had just been born to their heifer. "It was laying there kicking and my dad was walking away with a hammer," she said. "He had killed it. I ran to my mother, just bawling, because I just couldn't imagine him doing that. My mom looked at me and she said, 'He had to. We've just got the one milk cow. There's not enough milk for you kids and the calf too. You kids have got to have milk.' So he killed the calf."

To supplement their meager diet, her family scavenged whatever they could find,

including the weed lamb's-quarter, which the children picked in the dry creek beds. Virginia's mother experienced a windfall when a cousin with a steady job as a mail carrier presented her with a hundred baby chickens and five sacks of feed to get them started. But one night the brooder house caught on fire and the chickens perished. In the red glow of the disaster, Virginia saw her mother "trying to stand out of the light where we couldn't see her, but she was just sobbing like her heart was broken, cause that was another one of her dreams that had just gone away. But I remember the next morning, she fixed pancakes for us kids and said, 'We haven't had pancakes in a long time.' And she started singing 'Walking in Sunlight.' She never mentioned the chickens again and we didn't either."

Desperate for work, Virginia's father took a carpentry job in Colorado, building a store for a grocer who could pay only in food, which her father brought home on weekends. "One time he brought a plate of prunes back," Virginia said, and her mother made a sour cream prune pie out of them. "And I remember my dad going back out to the car to go back to Colorado. My mother always cried whenever Dad left—and if Mama cried, us kids cried. But I couldn't leave that prune pie, so I remember myself going in there and just eating that prune

Virginia Kerns Frantz's parents (top, left) did whatever they could to keep their family fed and clothed. Virginia (top, middle) wore dresses made from three feed sacks. Imogene Davison Glover (with her brother, top, right) wore flour sack dresses and panties made from sugar sacks. Her little brother got in trouble for swallowing two dimes their mother needed to buy food.

pie and just crying like everything. But I couldn't stop on the prune pie."

Mothers made do with whatever was at hand to feed their children. Some took the leftover oatmeal from breakfast and then fried it for the same day's dinner. A paste of flour, water, salt, and pepper—called "Kansas gravy"—was used to make noodles, or poured over toast to make a meal. Like many families, Clarence Beck's had a milk cow and egg-laying hens. "We sold both the milk and the cream, until the cow went dry, and eggs, except for the minimum that we could eat," he said. "The money we got was to buy staples—salt, flour, and lard. That wasn't enough. So you'd start borrowing from the grocer to the extent he'd lend you. And when he would quit lending you money, you were down to eating lard and bread. We ate so poorly that the hobos wouldn't come to our house."

Calvin Crabill's mother wanted a loaf of bread from the country store a half mile from their home, "and we looked for a dime in the house. We couldn't find a dime to buy a loaf of bread. Not a dime in the house."

Imogene Davison Glover was luckier. "It was rare for anyone to have money," she said, but one day her grandfather gave her three dimes:

And I was rich! I hid 'em. My mother wanted to know where. I said, "Well, I buried 'em in the sand out around the south window." And she said, "Well, you come show me." And she looked until she found those three dimes.

One time my brother swallowed two dimes, and my mother made him use a can or a slop jar to go to the bathroom until she dug those dimes out. So it was hard times.

Imogene's mother was resourceful in other ways. She made Imogene some new panties out of sugar sacks and dresses from

To boost sales, seed and flour distributors like the Sunbonnet Sue flour mill in Kansas (opposite) put their products in brightly decorated bags that housewives could sew into clothing for their children, which sometimes meant many girls, like those in Hickok, Kansas (below), showed up to school in the same designs.

flour sacks: "It wasn't good percale, it was just cotton that had been printed with little flowers on the sugar sacks. And that's why they were used for my panties. And the flour sacks might be plaid or have big flowers, and that's why they made dresses out of 'em." Virginia Kerns Frantz said that a new dress required three feed sacks, and once feed companies realized that farmers' wives might use them for their daughters' clothes, "they made them real pretty. We found out some of the neighbors wore the same dress as we did, but we always laughed at each other and went on because we had a new dress and it was fine."

South of Boise City, Don Wells and his family were struggling to survive on a

160-acre farm. "We didn't have anything," he said. "We were so poor we couldn't even pay attention. There were ten of us kids and we lived in a two-room house. At night we had wall-to-wall mattresses. At daytime we scooted them under the bed. We had two rooms—a kitchen and there was a bed in there, and the rest of us all slept in the other room. There weren't any storm windows. The houses didn't have any insulation and the houses weren't any good. We got the dust out of our house with a shovel."

Then, on Black Sunday, the Wells children learned that their father had died in the nearest hospital, 50 miles away, from what had started as strep throat and ended with him choking to death. (The date of the father's death was one daughter's birthday; the date of his funeral was another daughter's birthday.) Wells's mother, age thirty-five, was now a widow with a grade-school education and ten mouths to feed. "We couldn't stay out on the farm, 'cause the bank came and got what little machinery we had, which didn't amount to anything, but I'm sure it was mortgaged," he said. "And we didn't have any cows left. We didn't have any pigs to eat. So my uncles loaded us up in a truck—one truck, not a

Don Wells's family posed for a formal portrait in the better years before his father died on Black Sunday (top, left; Don is in the front with bow tie). Several years later, some of the children posed again (left; Don in white shirt and hat) in front of a house that wasn't theirs; they now lived in the chicken coop in the distant background.

At the Godown Mercantile in Boise City (above), Roy Godown paid farmers 5 cents a dozen cash for eggs—7 cents if they decided to exchange the eggs for goods in his store, where men's overalls cost 79 cents and a dozen oranges 19 cents. Godown was known for being kindhearted, allowing some families without items to barter to run up $500 in credit.

big truck, but a little truck—put all of our clothes and furniture in the back of it and they took us to Boise City."

His mother managed to get a job washing dishes at a local café, and an older sister went to work for a doctor. The family lived in one house after another, forced to move whenever they couldn't pay the rent, until they finally found something they could afford, Wells said:

> It was a chicken house. They had to get the chickens out of it and clean it up a little bit before we moved into it. We put windows in it and then, you know, of course cleaned it out real good. And they hung a little bit of wallpaper and stuff.

> But that's how things were. That tough, you know. There just wasn't any money, that's all there was to it.

> When we moved to town, we got commodities—a lot of prunes, which I hate to this day, and powdered milk. I remember those two things, and pinto beans, I remember those.

Townspeople were hit as hard as the farm families. With cash difficult to come by, many merchants conducted their business through barter. The newspaper in Hugoton, Kansas, accepted chickens in exchange for subscriptions. The movie theater in another small town took in eggs (valued at a penny each) as payment for admission. A Garden City family paid off its debt to a drugstore with milk (5 cents a quart) that was used for the soda fountain's shakes. After their three-year-old daughter died, another family supplied the funeral home with hams over a number of years to cover their bill.

Down in Amarillo, the Dust Bowl's biggest city, Pauline Durrett Robertson's father had been a prosperous businessman, with a wife and three daughters. "My father owned an insurance company," Pauline said, "and up until 1930, it was going fine. Then it began to falter because people couldn't afford insurance. It went into the hands of the receiver, they always said; I never did know what that meant. But it meant we didn't have a business anymore. So then he had to find work elsewhere and

When her father lost his business and his health, Pauline Durrett Robertson's mother (far left) had a nervous breakdown, leaving Pauline (in the darker dress,) and her sisters in charge of themselves and their father's care.

that was hard." He had a college education, but he was already in his fifties, and jobs were scarce. Then his health began to fail, making it even more difficult to find work. "And my mother began to despair that things were never going to get better, that in fact they were getting worse," Pauline recalled, the emotional pain of the story fresh in her mind:

> It affected her outlook on life and she began to—well she had a nervous breakdown actually, and was hospitalized. So we three girls were pretty motherless during the Depression.
>
> At one time, when we didn't have anything to eat, we had to apply for relief. That was hard for us to do, the three girls. And the brown truck with the marking on the side came to the front of our house and brought some food. And it was really hard for us to see that. I guess we were sorry for the neighbors to see that we needed that brown truck.

In some counties, the names of families on relief were published each month in the local newspaper. For those receiving cash subsidies, rules prohibited the money from being spent on soft drinks, ice cream, or movie tickets; it was restricted to rent, food staples, clothing, and medical care. "We could go to the courthouse in Beaver and get commodities if we wanted to," Pauline Arnett Hodges said. "The problem was that people like my father and some of our neighbors were too proud to go do that. And I remember my mother raising such a ruckus because *she* wasn't too proud. And we did get some grapefruit and some other kinds of commodities that helped out with food."

Despite the social stigma, by 1935 the number of families relying on some form of government assistance in counties throughout the Dust Bowl ranged from 25 to 80 percent of the population. The state and county governments were simultaneously overwhelmed and underequipped to meet the crisis; organizations like the Red Cross, American Legion, Ladies' Aid Society, and Gloom Chasers Club did their best to fill in, but could only have small-scale successes. Most of the help came from Washington and the flurry of New Deal programs President Roosevelt was creating to provide a lifeline for Americans living on the edge.

Fresh out of Colorado College with a degree in sociology, at age twenty-one Dorothy Christenson Williamson was hired as a social worker by the Federal Emergency Relief Administration (FERA) and dispatched to Prowers County in southeastern Colorado. She was assigned a 50-square-mile territory and went from one dust-ravaged farm to another, explaining the programs that provided surplus commodities, blankets, and other necessities to destitute families. "These people were so needy and you felt so sorry for them," she said. "You might feel like giving them a dollar out of your own pocket, but you just didn't do things like that. It's not 'professional'—you're not supposed to be that friendly when you're a caseworker. You're supposed to be business-like and ask questions and they're supposed to answer. But you couldn't help but feel really sorry for them and kind of helpless yourself." Decades later, at age ninety-seven, she said her conversations with the people she had met were still burned into her memory:

So we sat across the table and talked to each other. And it was almost as if they were in the middle of something that they could see no way out. That's why they looked so hopeless, and also they looked stunned as if, "Can this really be happening?" I think they began to feel that maybe it was never gonna be any better, that they had lost hope that anything would change. So it was a depressing atmosphere.

I remember this one man in particular—sitting across the table from him. It wasn't a conversation exactly. We talked about commodities and what they needed, that kind of thing. But there was always this feeling of, "We're glad you're trying to help, but nobody can help us." And so they had this look about them like people who have given up.

It left me with a bad feeling, too, to have to go out there and see these people, because you felt you were helping them as best you could, but you really couldn't help them. We could give 'em this little tiny bit of commodities, which helped them keep going, but there was no way

Dorothy Christenson Williamson (below, right) went to work as a caseworker in southeastern Colorado, explaining federal relief programs to farmers (like the one below) who often seemed dazed and without hope.

we could change their lives. There was no way we could change the situation they were in. There was no way you could stop the dust.

They needed this little bit of food and blankets, maybe that they got. But what they really needed was an inner thing that nobody could give them. They needed a trust again in something, which they had lost.

"We are fighting desperately to maintain our homes, schools, churches, and various enterprises to meet local needs," said a telegram signed by 1,500 people and sent to Washington. "We don't want dole or direct relief. We want work." Roosevelt's New Deal had programs for that, too.

The Civilian Conservation Corps (CCC) put young men to work in national parks, state parks, and national forests, and paid them $30 a month, $25 of which they were required to send home to their families.

The National Youth Administration (NYA), open to both boys and girls, let students remain at home and earn a little money through work-study projects. In Amarillo, Pauline Durrett Robertson was paid 25 cents an hour to grade papers. (Pauline also served as the editor of the school paper, *The Sandstorm*.) In Boise City, Don Wells and his older brother stayed after school to help the janitor clean classrooms. As a bonus, he let them take showers in the locker room—a luxury for boys who lived in a chicken coop without running water.

Lorene Delay White's father worked for the WPA building a bridge near Elkhart, Kansas (bottom), that is still in use; Pauline Arnett Hodges's father's WPA crew constructed the first paved road in No Man's Land (below). Even making WPA signs (below, left) created a job for someone who needed one.

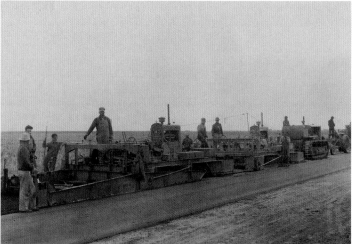

Marion Coen (above) found work with the CCC, sending most of his paycheck back to his parents and siblings (above, right); another brother got a WPA job building a new courthouse in Elkhart.

In southwestern Kansas, Lorene Delay White and her family relied on three different government programs. Lorene and her sister made $6 a month from the NYA for helping in the school lunchroom. Through FERA, her mother was provided with a pressure cooker to help preserve what food she could grow in the family garden. And Lorene's father reluctantly enrolled with the WPA, the Works Progress Administration, the New Deal's biggest—and most controversial—program.

"My dad was a proud man," Lorene said, "and he didn't want anything to do with government programs. He thought he could handle it on his own. He found out later that he needed to take part in them." He swallowed his pride and went to work for the WPA for a year, building a bridge over the North Fork of the Cimarron River for about 39 cents an hour, she said: "And one day my dad's car wouldn't start and he needed to get there and it was probably five miles over to the bridge. And I remember it was in the winter and he walked. He walked to get there because he needed to be there to work." (Nearly eighty years later, she proudly pointed out

that the bridge he built is still in use. "It's a beautiful bridge," she said.)

During the depths of the Depression, the WPA became the largest employer in the nation, creating 8 million jobs in virtually every corner of the country. "The prairie, once the home of the deer, buffalo, and antelope," one newspaper wrote, "is now the home of the Dust Bowl and the WPA." Many people considered it makework and a waste of money, saying the initials stood for "We're Probably Asleep."

"It made a lot of difference which side you were on," said Wayne Lewis. "If you didn't have a job [with the WPA], they were boondoggles—do-nothings, folks leaning on their shovels and getting money for it. And so they resented it very much. But if you were the ones that had the shovel, it was the difference between starving and having food to eat. It saved us; it kept us alive." Lewis's father, in Beaver County, Oklahoma, got a job with the WPA hauling dirt with his team and wagon on a road improvement project. One week, he let Wayne skip school for a few days to drive the horses and get paid for it. "And so I got to buy some new clothes," he said.

Reaping the Whirlwind **113**

"We would have starved to death because we had no other way to make any money," said Pauline Arnett Hodges. "The New Deal for us—the farm programs, but the WPA in particular—was just a lifesaver for us. Most of our neighbors felt that way. You couldn't have heard a bad word about Roosevelt anywhere." Millard Fowler, who made $4 to $5 a day when he brought his team of horses to work on road projects near Boise City, agreed. "We thought Roosevelt was a pretty good guy," he said, "because he was keepin' us alive."

During its eight-year history, the WPA undertook 1,410,000 projects, built 651,087 miles of highways and roads, and constructed or improved 124,031 bridges, 125,110 public buildings, 8,192 parks, and 853 landing fields.

Within the Dust Bowl, Pauline Arnett Hodges's father helped the WPA build Highway 64 through the Oklahoma Panhandle, which passed within a few miles to the south of Caroline Henderson's homestead. Harry Forester joined a crew working on roads just north of her. Boise City's projects included a new county courthouse, a city park, and a high school. In Elkhart, Kansas, Floyd and Dale Coen's oldest brother was paid to work on a new

courthouse, while another brother joined the CCC; their father wasn't permitted to hold a WPA job because he owned land that wasn't mortgaged. A dam was constructed on Rita Blanca Creek near Dalhart, Texas, to create a reservoir and recreation area. Bridges, culverts, a courthouse, a town park, and at least five schools went up in Baca County, Colorado.

But no part of the Dust Bowl put the WPA and other New Deal programs to more extensive use than Union County, New Mexico, thanks to its superintendent of schools, Raymond Huff. With the county on its economic knees, Huff decided to build a brand-new high school in the county seat of Clayton, along with a new gymnasium, athletic field, and vocational shops. And he persuaded WPA officials in Denver to let him organize the entire community to take on the job.

In the beginning, 600 people were put to work. Native stone was quarried and cut for the building; the lumber was cut and sawn nearby. Artisans were brought in to train townspeople, farmers, and students in other crafts. The school's rugs and drapes were made from wool clipped from Union County sheep, and colored with dyes that came from local plants, according to

In Clayton, New Mexico, school superintendent Raymond Huff (above, far left) mobilized an array of New Deal programs to build a new high school (opposite) and equip it with furniture made by local WPA crews (above). Nearly 60 percent of the county's population received some employment in the project, and the result was a high school students attend to this day.

and found some kind of temporary employment in building it. And superintendent Raymond Huff would be remembered as "The Man Who Saved Union County."

"In this time of severe stress," homesteader Caroline Henderson noted in her letter to the Secretary of Agriculture, "Next to the enduring character of our people, credit must be given for the continued occupation of the Plains country to the various activities of the federal government. Without some such aid as has been furnished, it seems certain that large sections must have been virtually abandoned." And while she noted, "I did not vote for the New Deal," she wanted to set the record straight against some of the "wickedly unjust" accusations made against it:

> *If mere dollars were to be considered, the actually destitute in our section could undoubtedly have been fed and clothed more cheaply than the works projects that have been carried out. But in our national economy, manhood must be considered as well as money. People employed to do some useful work may retain their self-respect to a degree impossible under cash relief. . . .*

> *If we must worry so over the ruinous effects of "made work" on people of this type, why haven't we been worrying for generations over the character of the idlers to whom some accident of birth or inheritance has given wealth unmeasured, unearned, and unappreciated?*

AS THE DROUGHT AND DEPRESSION both tightened their grip, a young woman returned to her former home in the southern Plains. The daughter of a compulsive gambler, Sanora Babb had spent her childhood, during the prosperous years of the wheat boom, moving from one place to the next in the area around No Man's Land: Baca County, Colorado; Elkhart and Garden

ancient Pueblo Indian formulas. A local potter taught students to make all the dishes for the lunchroom, using clay from the area. All of the hinges, door handles, and lamps were hammered out of scrap metal that had been collected at the town dump or bought from locals. Just one of the one hundred large iron lanterns in the school's entryways would have cost the county $100 to purchase; instead, it cost $1.95. The girls in home economics classes were paid by the NYA to sew the drapes for the windows, and to hand-embroider linens for the lunchroom tables made in the school's woodworking shop.

Huff convinced the government to let him hire people to run a makeshift cannery in the high school's football stadium: meat from some of the cattle being culled from nearby ranches as part of a herd-reduction program was canned for distribution to local residents who needed the food. Then he put the cattle's hides to use, hiring people to tan them and craft them into the seats and backs of the school's handmade chairs.

By the time the project was done, Clayton, New Mexico, had a fully equipped high school that would still be in use three-quarters of a century later. Nearly 6,000 of the 10,000 area residents had taken part

City, Kansas; and then Forgan, Oklahoma, where she had graduated from high school as the class valedictorian a decade earlier. (Town matrons, however, organized to prohibit Sanora from delivering the valedictory speech because she was "the gambler's daughter.")

After a job as cub reporter for the *Garden City Herald* in Kansas, she had moved to Los Angeles in 1929, hoping to make a name for herself on a big-city newspaper. The stock market crash and economic collapse had ended that dream, and she was homeless for a while, until she found temporary work in a string of secretarial jobs. In her free time, she began writing short stories.

When she came back for a brief visit with her mother, she could barely recognize her old hometown. "The little main street was quiet," she wrote. "No one came in and out of the stores. Four of the town's college graduates were sitting in the drugstore window. There wasn't any life anywhere. . . . From each end of the main street I could look out onto the drouth-desolated fields where no new crops were planted or would be planted this spring."

Even more startling was the way the catastrophe unfolding on the southern Plains had seemingly leveled all the social distinctions she had felt so keenly as a young girl:

> *I saw them standing in line for the meat and potatoes of relief. I saw the people I used to know, who had lived*

Before she left the southern Plains to pursue her dream of becoming a writer, Sanora Babb (right, during the boom years of the mid-1920s) felt stigmatized by being "the gambler's daughter." When she returned for a visit in the mid-1930s, it seemed that all social distinctions had been obliterated, leaving everyone in the same boat: demoralized and standing in line for commodities or relief checks (opposite).

smugly in their imaginary strata—the best people who had bathtubs and cars, the middle ones who had bathtubs and white-collar jobs, the unacceptable ones who had no bathtubs [and] manual jobs or doubtful means of support—standing in line together. . . . Their stricken faces, one after another in the line, looked very much alike.

There is something now they cannot get their hands on. "It don't seem right," they say, "when a man can't work for his livin'." Their cars are gone, their stock, their houses, their land, their money, their work, and they come into the town or out of its houses and fall in line for the meat and potatoes of relief.

This was just one little town, but I thought of all the other towns I had known and not known in the sections of Texas, New Mexico, Colorado, and Kansas that seam this strip of Oklahoma, and all the towns everywhere with their people gathering into the tight knots of distress and painful wonder at this unending process of decay that levels their lives down to a single want and fear.

They have nothing to look forward to this year and the next but relief. In the blind groping, some of them talk of migrating to other states, thinking to escape the drouth area they may escape depression. Where will they go in America to escape?

Sanora Babb returned to her new life in California, but she could not shake the memories of the proud yet helpless people she had known under different circumstances in her youth, before the southern Plains were known as the Dust Bowl.

Soon enough, she would see many of them again.

Chapter 7

GRAB A ROOT AND GROWL

Sure things are tough, the dust is terrible, the wheat is gone, the prospect for a row crop is diminishing and all hell's broke loose, but we know what is back of this country.

We know what it will do when it gets half a chance. We know that it will rain again and the High Plains always bounces back like Antaeus of mythical fame, stronger after each fall.

Grab a root and growl—hang on and let's see how this all comes out.

—*John L. McCarty*
Editor, Dalhart Texan

BOTH JOHN McCARTY and the Texas Panhandle town of Dalhart were less than thirty years old when he took over the *Dalhart Texan* in 1929. With the Great Plow Up still in full swing, the future seemed unlimited. But six years later, many people in town were losing hope. "My faith, for the first time, is being shaken in this country," the president of the local bank admitted. "We need somebody to save us from ourselves."

McCarty volunteered for the role. He was not going to let a little thing like a Great Depression or an unrelenting drought dim his ambitions. Having learned that advertisers preferred good news in the local paper, he happily provided it. "Aside from wind and sandstorms," he assured his readers, "there is really no disagreeable weather in the north Panhandle."

He organized a "Rally Against Dust" and 700 people showed up. Every time the slightest rain fell, he predicted the drought was finally ending. In early April of 1935, he ran a two-page picture of his adopted town with the caption: "Beautiful panoramic view of Dalhart shows it as a city of homes where living is a real pleasure." The next week, the massive storm of Black Sunday struck and buried the town in dust.

McCarty was unbowed. Under a headline proclaiming, "Foreign Dust Proves Panhandle Irritant," he pointed out that the dirt causing all of Dalhart's problems had blown in from other states. And the people in those places, he said, were a "bunch of sissies, softies, and crybabies" because they complained so much and kept looking for someone else to help them. But not his loyal readers. "It has appeared that the hate of all nature has been poured out against us," he told them, but they were as tough as the toughest people in the history of Western civilization: "Spartans!

John L. McCarty at his typewriter at the *Dalhart Texan*.

Preceding pages:
A farmer surveys a country road and his fields, all smothered in dirt, 1935.

Like every other town in the Dust Bowl, Dalhart, Texas (above), was battered by the constant dirt storms and deepening economic Depression; but John McCarty kept up a steady outpouring of upbeat news, like his "A Tribute to Dalhart" (above, far right), which said the town had "more iron nerve, more he-man guts and more patient courage than any other place in the world."

No better word can describe the citizens of the north Plains country of Dalhart. Bravery and hardship are but tools out of which great empires are carved and real men [are] made Spartans."

In his hyperbolic boosterism, even the weather plaguing his "Spartans" was worthy of McCarty's praise:

> Hail to our sandstorms! The beauty that was Greece, the glory that was Rome, the undying honor that was due those immortal heroes at the Alamo . . . are as nothing compared with the genuine Panhandle dust storm.
>
> Yesterday . . . one of those magnificent spectacles of nature bounded upon Dalhart out of the Northwest. It was inspiring, as the giant gray sand clouds surged and boiled forward across the plains, leaving the more slowly advancing purple wall of dust behind.
>
> Then for hours the dust of many states fell like a heavy snow upon the town, one soft, ebony chalk sheet after another settling until it seeped through every crevice and settled into every tiny crack. . . . Like the fog of London, it penetrated everything.
>
> Let us pay a tribute to our sandstorms. Since we have them, let us recognize their true worth, their real beauty and the dramatic power they exert as a force of nature. Let us proclaim with clarion bugle blasts heard round the world that we have here in the Panhandle a spectacle of nature that rolls more majestic than the mighty Niagara, that sweeps onward with a power far greater than the Father of the Waters, and for its awful splendor, its terrible manifestation of the dark mood of nature, raped and wronged by man, exceeds anything short of the mighty oceans or the barren icy wastes of the polar regions.
>
> Let us praise nature and the powerful God that rules nature. Let us in stentorian tones boast of our terrific and mighty sandstorms and of a people, a city, and a country that can meet the test of courage they afford and still smile . . . smile, even though we may be choking and our throats and nostrils so laden with dust that we cannot give voice to our feelings.

To help God and nature along a little, McCarty, now doubling as the director of the Dalhart Chamber of Commerce, decided in 1935 to pass the hat and hire someone who could make it rain. For $300, Tex Thornton promised to send sticks of dynamite aloft and detonate them every ten minutes. The percussions would shake the moisture out of the skies, he claimed, just as the heavy artillery bombardments of World War I seemed to have resulted in the troops spending so much time in rain-drenched trenches.

On May 1, just a couple weeks after Black Sunday, several thousand eager onlookers gathered 4 miles south of Dalhart to watch Thornton attach his TNT and nitroglycerin jelly to balloons, in preparation for the assault on the low clouds overhead. McCarty and other businessmen had scheduled a street dance for that evening to celebrate the expected downpour. But a dust storm swept over them all, driving the spectators to their cars. Unable to release his balloons in the brisk wind, Thornton buried his explosives in the ground and detonated them—sending even more dirt into the air. No rain.

Two more days of noisy explosions were equally ineffective. But the night after his fourth attempt, a slight amount of precipitation fell. Thornton and McCarty—ignoring the fact that Denver, Albuquerque, and Kansas, far away from the pyrotechnics, got even more precipitation on the same day— claimed victory. "I'm mighty glad that the people of Dalhart and the Panhandle got moisture," Thornton said before picking up his money and leaving town, "and if I had anything to do with it, I'm doubly glad."

Dalhart boosters scheduled a party to celebrate the rainmaker's success (above), but instead all they got was more dust (top).

In a barren field stripped of most vegetation, soil scientist H. Howard Finnell contemplates the daunting challenge of "Operation Dust Bowl."

Our efforts to manipulate the forces of nature to fit our own convenience are wrong. Instead we should attempt to harmonize our farming operations to fit conditions as they are rather than as we hope they will be.

—*H. Howard Finnell*

H. HOWARD FINNELL had arrived in Dalhart on a very different mission from that of rainmaker Tex Thornton—and he would stay much longer. Finnell was a soil scientist, with a degree from Oklahoma A&M, and for ten years he had been running the agricultural experiment station in Goodwell, Oklahoma, about 25 miles south of Caroline Henderson's homestead. There he had embarked on a series of studies on better ways to grow crops in the semiarid southern Plains, meticulously keeping track of everything he did in a small journal.

Under typical farming methods, he concluded, nearly 80 percent of a year's rainfall never soaked deeply enough into the subsoil to benefit the crops. As a result, wheat farmers could expect only four good harvests out of every ten, even during normal weather conditions. "I realize that agriculture is something of a gamble from the time a man plants his seed until he brings a crop to harvest," he wrote, "but I can see no necessity for this kind of gambling. . . . The economics of soil conservation are based not on one year, or even ten years, but in the long run—on many years, even centuries."

In his experiments—some based on suggestions by old-timers with long experience on the Plains—Finnell had discovered techniques to double the odds of a good crop by capturing as much moisture as possible: using terraces and plowing along the land's contour to minimize runoff; keeping, rather than stripping, plant residues on the surface after a harvest; planting different crops, depending on subsoil conditions; and making deeper rows with the plow called a lister, rather than pulverizing the soil with the more popular one-way plow.

"We do not want a changed climate," Finnell wrote. "All that is needed to reach a solution of many of the drouth problems is to make a better use of the rain that is received. Moisture conservation is the answer."

In the space of a decade, Finnell had published fifty-nine reports of his findings, but few farmers paid much attention to his recommendations. It was the 1920s, times were good, and they were more interested in finding additional grassland to plow.

But Finnell's work did catch the eye of Hugh Bennett, the head of the newly created Soil Conservation Service, who quickly hired him and put him in charge of one of the agency's largest and hardest hit regions in the nation: nearly 100 million acres of the southern Plains—an area four times the size of Ohio. Finnell's first task was to set up some demonstration projects north of Dalhart, where he hoped to prove to skeptical farmers that his techniques were worth following. He persuaded a handful of owners to sign three-year contracts agreeing to cooperate; the government would pay for the work, and any improvements made during that time would belong to the landowner.

It was called "Operation Dust Bowl" and a lot was riding on the results. In 1935, an estimated 850 million tons of topsoil were being swept off the naked fields of the Plains, where 4 million acres, in 101 counties, were blowing. Predictions called for a million more acres to do the same thing in 1936. One report said the Dust Bowl was expanding eastward at 30 miles a year, and predicted that even cities on the East Coast might ultimately be buried in dust, like some ancient civilizations. "Unless something is done," another report concluded, "the western plains will be as arid as the Arabian desert."

HOMESTEADING IN REVERSE: An abandoned farm north of Dalhart (opposite). Farmers signing papers (above) or waiting to sign (above, right) to sell their land back to the federal government through the Resettlement Administration, one of FDR's most controversial agricultural programs. Most of the land was then taken out of production and reseeded as grasslands.

"There were many people who thought this is not going to stop with western Kansas, the Texas Panhandle; it's going to start creeping eastward," said historian Donald Worster. "That is, this is a process that will just unravel all across America. And so how do you stop this? What's going to be the barrier you put up to keep it from undermining agriculture in Illinois?"

Within President Roosevelt's inner circle of advisers, there was no consensus on what to do about the crisis. Henry Wallace, the Secretary of Agriculture, and Hugh Bennett thought new policies could keep farmers on their land. But Interior Secretary Harold Ickes questioned whether any attempt should be made to save the Dust Bowl. "It was a character struggle within the administration the same way it was a character struggle out on the prairie itself," said writer Timothy Egan. "Ickes says, 'Let's just get out. Let's pull out. Mr. President, it's not worth the effort. Why should we try to save the people or the land? Let's not fool these people into thinking they can stay there.' I mean, let it re-wild."

Another New Deal program, the Resettlement Administration, was already buying up farms on the most marginal lands, taking it out of production and providing the displaced farmers with loans of up to $700 to encourage them to move

somewhere else. It was a controversial program; most people in the region despised it. "It was homesteading in reverse," Egan explained. "It was an acknowledgement that we failed, that settlement itself was perhaps an accident of history. Perhaps people weren't even meant to live there, let alone farm there."

One Resettlement official suggested that simply ending all forms of federal relief would create a stronger incentive to get people off the land. But Roosevelt refused to go that far. He wanted as many as possible to remain. He was just as much a "next year" person as the farmers of the Plains. (His favorite American song, Roosevelt said, was "Home on the Range," especially the lines saying, "Where seldom is heard a discouraging word, and the skies are not cloudy all day.") "I think Roosevelt really had a soft spot for American farmers," historian Donald Worster said, "and he saw this as a vital foundation that needed to be saved."

The program closest to the president's heart was one that he had suggested himself—planting rows of trees up and down the Great Plains as windbreaks to reduce the ferocity of the storms. "Roosevelt believed in trees," according to Worster. "Trees were his religion you might say. He was sure that planting trees would stop

this deserts-on-the-march problem, would rehabilitate the country, would make everything pleasant for people living on these farms. So he instituted a major shelterbelt program that would plant trees from Canada all the way down into Texas."

Roosevelt's plan was ridiculed by many; even some members of his administration doubted that the project would succeed. But the president was insistent, and young men in the Civilian Conservation Corps were soon put to work planting seedlings on farms whose owners agreed to participate. One eleven-man team could plant 6,000 trees a day. By the end of the decade, the program would account for 18,600 miles of shelterbelts with 217 million trees. (In Nebraska, an ancient, gnarled tree was cut down. A study of its rings revealed that it was nearly 750 years old, and during that time the Great Plains had suffered twenty

FDR'S PET PROJECT: President Roosevelt insisted on a program of planting trees as windbreaks and shelterbelts up and down the Great Plains. CCC crews (opposite, bottom) often did the work, and then landowners (opposite, top) were responsible for the trees' care. In the spring of 1937, Floyd S. Moon of Pratt, Kansas, began his own shelterbelt in cooperation with the government (right) and then posed with the result seven years later (below).

droughts similar in severity to the one under way in the 1930s.)

Since most of the shelterbelts were actually planted east of the Dust Bowl, where they had better chances of surviving, they provided little help for the hardest hit areas. "It went through central Kansas," Worster said. "I think it had some effects there. It was certainly a beautification of the landscape in many ways. It provided great shelterbelts for birds and wildlife. It probably cut some wind erosion down. But it had no effect farther west, because trees won't grow there."

If the shelterbelts weren't as dramatically effective as Roosevelt had hoped in stopping the fields of the Dust Bowl from blowing, Howard Finnell saw a different

benefit to the program, focused closer to the farmers' homes. "In addition to controlling erosion on the farmstead area," he wrote, "such windbreaks will make it possible to develop a real farm home and encourage a permanent rural population. By so doing, farmstead windbreaks will remove one of the main causes of wind erosion—the farmer who is interested only in mining the soil and moving on to a better place to live."

Meanwhile, in Dalhart, Finnell was getting to work on the demonstration project of his own ideas. "A stupendous mistake was made," he admitted, when so much grassland unsuited for farming was stripped of its natural cover during the Great Plow Up. But he thought those areas could be stabilized and reseeded as pastures. At the same time, much of the land with better soils could still produce crops, he believed, if the farmers would only change their attitudes:

> *The fundamental cause of our erosion problem [is] the reckless denudation of the soil. Now, slowly and painfully, we must undertake to retrace our steps . . . where unwise agricultural practice has brought us face to face with a land catastrophe.*

> *The great dictator in the High Plains is Nature. Man, in order to keep a viable, healthy, and permanent civilization in this region, must discover a system of farming which is so adapted to Nature as to maintain a productive soil . . . a type of agriculture [that is] stable through droughts as well as during periods of abundant precipitation.*

Howard Finnell took this photograph of two barren trees, with the soil at their roots scoured away and sand dunes in the distance, then placed it in a report to his superiors to demonstrate the magnitude of the crisis.

John L. McCarty created the Last Man Club, with rallies (top) and special membership cards (above) to strengthen people's resolve to persevere on their land.

It seems certain that if a permanent type of agriculture is ever to be established on cultivated land where the rainfall is low, a revolutionary change in methods of water conservation and in crop management is required.

"Finnell believed that people had a choice; you could do the right thing or you could do the wrong thing," said agricultural historian R. Douglas Hurt. "And the right thing would be sensibly making the kinds of adjustments that he knew would work. He really believed that even though drought is inevitable, it doesn't have to be catastrophic."

Dalhart's biggest booster, John L. McCarty, had come up with his own plan to keep people from leaving. In a classic publicity stunt, he proclaimed the formation of the Last Man Club, to be comprised of people who promised to stick it out on the Plains with McCarty until, as he put it, "hell freezes over." Several hundred signed up, including Finnell and even the governor of Texas.

"I saw a cow leaning against a big telegraph pole yesterday, nibbling away the short grass showing up through the sand," McCarty wrote in his column, *Old Loco*, "a cow so thin she had to lean up against a telephone pole to keep from blowing away and yet still [with] enough guts, hope, faith, and courage to nibble around the sand for short grass. If I could get her pedigree, number, and name, I'd enroll that cow in my Last Man Club. She had the old Dalhart spirit."

But despite John McCarty's exhortations, Howard Finnell's scientific promises, and President Roosevelt's cheery optimism, thousands of families throughout the Dust Bowl were facing an excruciating decision: In the land that once held such a boundless future for them, was there any future left? Could they survive another year in "next year" country?

Chapter 8

CANAAN LAND

You go broke gradually. It doesn't happen like jumping off of a cliff. You exhaust your savings; you exhaust your borrowings; you exhaust your equipment; you exhaust yourself—and you give up.

Then you're starting to look at the wolves. And that takes about five years.

—*Clarence Beck*

CLARENCE BECK'S PARENTS, Sam and Nora, had moved from northern Kansas to a farm near Wheeless, Oklahoma, just west of Boise City, as the 1920s were ending. The land and house were owned by relatives, but Clarence's father hoped to do well enough to buy a farm of his own.

His timing couldn't have been worse. By 1935, he had suffered repeated crop failures because of the unending drought, and the economic Depression meant there were no jobs, though he found temporary work with the WPA to keep his family from starvation. Like many other families, they talked about starting over somewhere else. "People didn't leave earlier because there was no place to go," Clarence said. "Where can you go when you're penniless? At least where you are, you have the feel-at-homeness; you know everything that's around you."

Meanwhile, the hard times placed a strain on Sam and Nora's marriage. "My mother would have been a playgirl, really," Clarence explained. "And my father was a drudge. He would be perfectly happy to work from dawn till dusk. My mother would never want to work. She would have loved to have had a little money and done the town every night or so."

"She liked to dance and she liked to go out," said her daughter, Irene Beck Hauer, Clarence's younger sister. "She really didn't care to be on a farm and in a home, to can fruit and do things. That wasn't her type. She didn't care for it."

One morning, before Irene headed for school, her mother took her aside to deliver some news:

> *She just said "I won't be home when you come home tonight from school. I won't be home. I'm leavin'." My mother went with her sister, my aunt, and just left.*

> *So that was it. She didn't care about me that much or anything. She went back to Kansas with her sister.*

Not long afterward, a different type of disaster struck. Their father's tractor—the only possible means for him to stay on the land—was repossessed. "That," Clarence

Preceding pages:
Dust Bowl refugees from Oklahoma on their way to new lives in California.

Abandoned by their mother, Clarence Beck and his sister, Irene (below), were split apart when their father lost his farm west of Boise City and headed to California with Irene, leaving Clarence with uncles in central Kansas.

The nine Forester children lined up at their grandmother's house in Goodwell, Oklahoma: William (front row, left) was the youngest and Robert (front row, middle) a little older. Louise (front row, right) had become frightened by her father's despair, and redheaded Shirley (middle row, right) was tired of being burned by the sun and sand.

remembered, "was the death knell to him as a farmer."

Sam Beck decided he had to move. Clarence would stay with uncles back in central Kansas, where he could continue his schooling. Irene wasn't sure what her father had in mind for her:

> At first I asked him, "Are you leavin' too?" I was kind of cryin', you know, 'cause naturally I was sad. So he said, "No, we're goin' to California."
>
> That kind of helped ease my mind. I wasn't happy about it, but I just thought, "At least I got a place to go." I thought, "At least he stood by me. He's nice enough to me and not leavin' me. Well, we're goin' to California."

Not that far from the Becks, in an adjoining county in the Oklahoma Panhandle, Harry Forester had lost his farm and was also living on someone else's land. He had once dreamed of prospering enough to give each of his five sons 640 acres. Now he could barely feed his nine children. His worries were impossible to keep secret from his kids. "One time he came in from the wind blowing and dust and he was pacing the floor because he'd come in from the plowing or whatever he was doing," said Louise Forester Briggs, one of his daughters. "And I remember him pacing the floor and saying, 'I don't know whatever will become of us.' And that just frightened me. My heart just clutched from that. So I didn't know what was gonna become of us either."

With his fields ruined by dust, and what was left of his livestock reduced to skin and bones, Forester had no choice but to give up farming. First he moved his large family to Goodwell, Oklahoma, where they could stay with his wife's mother. "After all the rest of the family had relocated to town to live at Granny's house, he stayed behind to kill the milk cows and the saddle horses and the draft horses," said William Forester, the youngest son. "There was no market for them. It was a very sad time for dad. He was dusted out and busted out."

Forester had read about a place where jobs were plentiful, where he could make good money and save enough to send for his family. He, too, would head to California.

In eastern Colorado, Calvin Crabill's father, John, was coming to the same conclusion. "My mother had asthma, and he was convinced that if he didn't get her out of there, she was going to die," said Calvin. "We had nothing left. There was no reason to stay. We lived in four different places when I was in elementary school to survive. Every year, my first, second, and third grade, we moved to a different farm, and every time we lost it. And so when we had nothing left, we left."

But first John Crabill had to sell his horses. "My mother and others who knew him said once he sold his horses he was never the same again the rest of his life," his son said. "He was probably about forty or forty-one when he sold all his horses. He never was the same again. He would be staring off into space and we knew he was thinking about his stock."

Not everyone who decided to leave chose California for a destination. Dorothy Sturdivan Kleffman's father thought he could hang on to his farm in Texas County, Oklahoma, but his wife had contracted dust pneumonia and couldn't stay. "I think she would have died," Dorothy said. "He could see that she was failing, and so he knew he had to do something." She added, "I really didn't wanna go. This was my home. And even though we had the dust storms and we were in a Great Depression, I would have loved to have just stayed right here. But because we had to save her life, we had to move."

Sturdivan and his oldest son would stay on the farm, but he moved his wife and younger children, including Dorothy, not to California, but east—to Arkansas, well out of the brown world of the Dust Bowl. For the children, arriving at a home with a green grass lawn was startling enough, Dorothy said, but for the chickens that had been brought along, "they would raise their legs up high [because] they were not used to that grass." In Arkansas, there was rain enough for her mother to raise a big garden ("we didn't have to water it like we did back home," Dorothy noted), and the children went to local orchards to pick pears and apples. All of it ended up in 600 quarts of

John Crabill (above, with Calvin) had to sell his horses before leaving Colorado for California—a loss that haunted him for the rest of his life.

Dorothy Sturdivan Kleffman's father (above) decided to stay on his Oklahoma farm, but his wife (with him, above right) had dust pneumonia, so he moved her and the younger children east, to Arkansas.

canned food their mother preserved. "But we wanted to come back," Dorothy said. "This was our home out here. We wanted to come back."

In Union County, New Mexico, Pauline Heimann Robertson's father was trying to talk his wife into leaving for central Kansas:

> Daddy said, "We can't stay here. Who knows how bad this is going to be? You wanna wait till we all starve? I mean we've got to do something. We have no choice. We've got to go." And that's when he decided to go to Kansas.
>
> Mother was not at all happy with goin'. And mother said, "I'm not at all wantin' to do this, but I just won't go without some chickens."
>
> And Daddy said, "Well, we'll take some chickens. How many chickens do you wanna take?"
>
> And she said, "At least a dozen. But what are we going to do haulin' chickens and kids and all of this in a car?"

Heimann built a crate, covered it with burlap, attached it to the front of their Dodge, and they left their home, with virtually all of their other belongings left behind. (What was left of his cattle herd was shipped by railroad.) The memory of leaving still brought tears to Pauline's eyes more than seventy years later: "It was bad. It was really bad. Because we didn't know where we were going, you know. I mean, we had no house, had nothin'. We mainly took the clothes that we wore. Mother and Daddy and two kids."

Outside of Boise City, they ran into a black blizzard that engulfed them in darkness. Sand and gravel peppered the car, pitting the windshield and scouring the paint off the fenders. Somehow, they made it through to their destination, where her father learned of a recently vacated house for rent. And the chickens, though undoubtedly traumatized by the storm, had managed to survive the 350-mile journey.

"It was a small house, but we got by with it just fine," Pauline said. "And out in the back in the neighbor's yard, they had

a chicken house. And Daddy said, 'Well, there's the chicken house. We'll just take the chickens and go put 'em over in the chicken house.'" As the family settled into their new surroundings, her father made them all a solemn promise:

> Daddy said all the time, "This'll be over one day. And when it is and the cattle can get enough to eat, we're going to be back."
>
> Daddy said we would come back to New Mexico as soon as it rained and it will. And he said, "When I see a thistle start growin', we'll be gettin' ready to move back to New Mexico."

In Boise City, Hazel Lucas Shaw was fretting over her recently born son, Charles. She had already lost her infant daughter, Ruth Nell, to the dust, and she was determined not to let it happen again. She hovered over her baby, covering his crib with a

They sold the funeral home, packed up, and moved east to Vici, in central Oklahoma, nearer to where Ruth Nell was buried. Hazel would stay there the rest of her life, although she always said she still missed the wide expanses of No Man's Land. "I remember my mother used to say even up into her later years, up until her nineties, and she lived to be ninety-nine, she used to say, 'Oh the wind's blowing tonight. I can sleep good,'" Charles said. "When she could hear the wind blow, she felt comfortable."

Some of our neighbors with small children, fearing the effects upon their health, have left temporarily "until it rains." Others have left permanently, thinking doubtless that nothing could be worse.

Thus far we and most of our friends seem held—for better or for worse—by memory and hope. I can look backward and see our covered wagon drawn up by the door of the cabin in the early light of that May morning long ago, can feel again the sweet fresh breath of the untrodden prairie, and recall for a moment the proud confidence of our youth.

But when I try to see the wagon—or the old Model T truck—headed in the opposite direction, away from our home and all our cherished hopes, I cannot see it at all. Perhaps it is only because the dust is too dense and blinding.

—*Caroline Henderson*

Pauline Heimann Robertson's family (opposite, bottom) pulled up stakes from New Mexico to central Kansas, driving 350 miles through fierce storms (opposite, top) with a crate of chickens on the front of their vehicle. In Boise City, Hazel Lucas Shaw now had another child, Charles Jr. (above), but she worried that he, too, would perish from the dust, so they moved to central Oklahoma.

wet sheet, vigilant about any change in his health. "If I coughed a little bit," Charles said, "she was all over me like ducks on a June bug."

But nothing Hazel could do seemed to keep the dirt from invading her home and threatening her son. Her husband's funeral home was suffering, too—not from a lack of business, but because bereaved families had no money to pay for his services. Much as she once loved the sweeping vistas of No Man's Land, where she had grown up and where most of her family still lived, Hazel could hold out no longer. "I don't know that it was the matter of being convinced with one event more than that the dust just kept on blowing," Charles said. "They didn't wanna take the chance of losing me, so they moved out."

CAROLINE AND WILL HENDERSON were staying put. But they couldn't ignore the evidence that others had given up. On a trip to get parts for their tractor that summer, from the road she observed "many pitiful reminders of broken hopes and apparently wasted effort. Little abandoned homes where people had drilled deep wells for the precious water, had set trees and

vines, built reservoirs, and fenced in gardens—with everything now walled in or half buried by banks of drifted soil—told a painful story of loss and disappointment."

Texas County, Oklahoma, where they had been homesteading since 1907, lost 30 percent of its population in the 1930s. Nearby Cimarron County lost 32 percent. Baca County, just across the line in Colorado, saw 41 percent of its residents move somewhere else.

Hardest hit was Morton County, Kansas, where Edgar and Rena Coen were raising their large family, now diminished by two with the deaths of a daughter and grandson from dust pneumonia. The Coens weren't leaving, but their county would lose nearly half of its population—and would close eleven of its seventeen rural schools—because the dust storms refused to relent. "You never got used to 'em," Floyd Coen said. "You just hated every one of 'em because you knew it was going to do damage outside. And you knew you were probably gonna lose some more neighbors. We were in school then, and one day your neighbors were there at school and next day they'd moved away. Kind of a sad time that way."

Leaving or staying, everyone had similar tales of sadness and heartbreak. "I remember when a neighbor left," Lorene Delay White said. "They lived just south of us and we played with their kids. And they came by, they had their truck loaded with all the possessions they could take with them. I think they had six kids. And I remember that made me feel lonely because they were gone."

Imogene Davison Glover watched her aunt, uncle, and cousins load what they could into a car and prepare to depart for California: "And the last thing Daddy said to my Uncle Jack was, 'Do you have enough money for gas to get there?' And Jack told him however much he had. And Daddy said, 'Well, I've just got seventeen dollars on me. But I want you to take this so you'll have enough money for gas.' And I thought, 'We probably won't ever see 'em again,' because we couldn't go to California. We didn't dream of going to California at that time."

For Pauline Arnett Hodges, the most vivid memory was of the strangers, not relatives, who left. "Every day, all day long, those cars passed our house," she said. "They often stopped and asked for food. We didn't

SAD FAREWELLS: A lonely boy outside his dust-ravaged house near Elkhart, Kansas (above, left); and Imogene Davison Glover's grandparents (above) who watched some of their children and grandchildren give up and move to the West Coast.

have very much, but my mother thought we were better off than other people, and we were because of the WPA. And she always fed them something. I still remember it was often bread and butter sandwiches, but it was something. She never, ever turned anybody down. I never saw that expression as I did on those people who were trying to get out of here—go someplace else to have a better life. I remember that several times, the women especially would cry and thank my mother for the bread and butter sandwiches."

In Beaver County, Oklahoma, just east of the Hendersons, Wayne Lewis remembered the diaspora through statistics he and his brother memorized in junior high school. "When I was in the eighth grade, we had a practical lesson in geography," he recalled. "How many people live in the district? And it was a hundred people. How many people are in school? Twenty-five. And then my brother got to the same place ten years later. How many people in the district? Twenty-five. How many kids in the school? Maybe ten. The rest of 'em had left."

But in the end, for every family that left the Dust Bowl, three families—75 percent of the population—would hang on.

"Our normal reaction to looking at what was happening in the 1930s is often to say, 'Well why didn't just everybody go?'" said cultural historian Pamela Riney-Kehrberg. "But it's a very complicated situation. If you owned your farm, picking up and moving was a very unpleasant option because more than likely you couldn't sell your farm. Nobody wanted to buy land in the Dust Bowl. And not only that but prices are severely depressed. And so the farm that you put your life into, that you put your blood, sweat, and tears into, is now worth nothing to anybody other than you. So picking up and moving means abandoning something that you had invested your life in. And people balanced that against the lack of opportunities elsewhere and said, 'Well, maybe the best thing to do is just to see if we can hang on a little longer.' And because of the federal farm programs, because of the relief programs, hanging on a little bit longer was possible."

SIGNS OF THE TIME: Some Dust Bowl counties lost nearly half of their population in the late 1930s, but on average three-quarters of the people determined to stick it out.

"The Plains can lay a hold on your affections if you're there for a generation or two," added Donald Worster. "They're a glorious place to live at times. The great skies and the openness and the sense of freedom—there were powerful draws for these people."

In one of her "Letters from the Dust Bowl," published in the *Atlantic Monthly*, Caroline Henderson asked and answered the same question in June 1935:

> *Naturally you will wonder why we stay where conditions are so extremely disheartening. Why not pick up and leave as so many others have done?*
>
> *I cannot act or feel or think as if the experiences of our twenty-seven years of life together had never been. And they are all bound up with the little corner to which we have given our continued and united efforts. To leave voluntarily—to break all these closely knit ties for the sake of a possibly greater comfort elsewhere— seems like defaulting on our task.*

> *We may have to leave. We can't hold out indefinitely without some return from the land. . . . But I think I can never go willingly or without pain that as yet seems unendurable.*
>
> *We long for the garden and little chickens, the trees and birds and wild- flowers of the years gone by. Perhaps if we do our part these good things may return some day, for others if not for ourselves.*

Still, despite the high percentage of Dust Bowl families like the Hendersons clinging to their land, there was no denying that a historic movement was under way— "one of the biggest folk migrations in American history," according to Donald Worster. "It dwarfs the movement along the Oregon Trail in the nineteenth century, the covered wagon era that we so idealize and romanticize. But we've forgotten this migration of the 1930s. Nobody celebrates it. We're ashamed of it basically because it was a migration of the defeated."

Most of them were headed to California

Not all the refugees heading west were from the Dust Bowl, but many passed through it on their way to California: An Arkansas family fixes a tire on their overloaded truck in Oklahoma (below) and another (below, left) crosses New Mexico.

on Route 66, joining an even larger exodus of Americans displaced by the Depression and the agricultural crisis that extended far beyond the Dust Bowl of the southern Plains. Oklahoma alone suffered a net migration loss of half a million people, but only 2 percent of them were from the westernmost tip ravaged by the black blizzards. The overwhelming number came from the more populous central and eastern parts of the state, where the crash in prices for cotton meant landowners were now kicking tenants off their farms. The same was true for Texas, Arkansas, and other states. At first, some federal officials, like Secretary of Labor Frances Perkins, encouraged the mass movement from the nation's heartland. "Large-scale emigration from the Great Plains is still necessary," she said, "to correct the previous oversettlement of this area."

"The Exodusters they were called, these refugees, were largely from the eastern fringe of the Dust Bowl; they were arguably not even from the Dust Bowl itself," said writer Timothy Egan. "They were Arkies from Arkansas. They were from Missouri. And they were tenant farmers, and when the farm economy collapsed, when the prices collapsed and you couldn't make a living, if you were a tenant farmer you had nothing, because you didn't even own the dirt. So they left."

"There was a river of people flowing into California in the 1930s," Donald Worster added. "They weren't all poor and they weren't all from the Great Plains. Some of them were fairly affluent; some of them were from Chicago. You can just see all of these cars pulling out from little side roads along the way, joining this brigade going out Route 66, stopping at motels, sleeping under billboards." Worster's own parents

A fully loaded—or overloaded—truck bears another family to a new beginning.

FAMILIES IN TRANSIT: A Texas family stays in the shade of their tarp while the father works on the truck's back axle (opposite, top), while another family piles out of their sedan to deal with a flat (opposite, bottom left); meanwhile one family's goat was deemed too essential to leave behind (opposite, bottom right). Tex Pace (in white cap, top right, with parents and brother) made three solo trips to California from the Texas Panhandle before he persuaded his family to join him on a permanent move in the "Promised Land."

were among them, leaving Kansas and getting as far as Needles, California, just across the Arizona state line, before deciding to stop and start their lives over there.

"These people didn't have but one thing to do and that was to just get out in the middle of the road," Woody Guthrie explained to folklorist Alan Lomax. "These people just got up, and they . . . bundled up their little belongings they throw'd in, one or two little things they thought they'd need. They had heard about the land of California, where you sleep outdoors at night, where you work all day in the big fruit orchards. You make enough to live on and get by on and live decent on, and you work hard, work honest. And according to the handbills they passed out down in that country, you're supposed to have a wonderful chance to succeed in California." Having survived the fury of Black Sunday in Pampa, Texas, Guthrie also answered California's siren song.

And Seth "Tex" Pace, recently graduated from high school in the Panhandle town of Briscoe, was working in a field on a sweltering summer day when he decided that he, too, had had enough. "All the time I was working in the hot, sweaty days and sandstorms, it's going through my mind, 'There's got to be a better way to make a livin'," he said. "And I thought, 'To make a better livin' I got to get out of here.'" He caught a ride with a friend, "going to the Promised Land," he laughed. "I couldn't wait to get to California." The day after arriving in Marysville, he began picking peaches for $5 a day. "I had never seen that much money in my life," he said. "I was rich."

Pace would migrate to California three times on his own—finding work picking fruit, delivering handbills, clerking in a store, washing dishes in a café—and each time he came home to Texas with some of the money he had made, even if it meant hopping freight trains to get from one place to the other. When the bank eventually took his father's farm, Pace convinced his parents to go with him on his fourth trip and relocate in California for good.

Meanwhile, in eastern Colorado, with the money from selling his horses in his pockets, Calvin Crabill's father loaded what he could into their small sedan and a little two-wheeled trailer, with Nanna the goat tied on top, and joined the stream of cars rattling down Route 66, with his eleven-year-old son and asthmatic wife, bound for southern California, where a family they knew lived. "When you came down that grade into San Bernardino and you saw the green valley there, that was a beautiful, beautiful sight," Calvin said. "You see the trees. My mother that day picked an orange, a ripe orange, and ate it. And that was something for her."

By now, Harry Forester was in Oakland, working a variety of jobs, sometimes making a dollar a day and sending as much of it as possible back to his wife and children in Goodwell, Oklahoma. Everything he held dear was half a continent away. The separation from his family made him miserable, and then came news from home that added to his woes: his brother- and sister-in-law had both died, and one of his five sons, Slats, who had been caught outside herding cattle on Black Sunday, had

come down with dust pneumonia. "My oldest brother was at death's door," Louise Forester Briggs said. "And my dad didn't know whether to come home or not, 'cause he thought Slats was gonna die. I imagine he was absolutely the loneliest man on the planet because he adored his family."

Forester decided his family should join him in Oakland as soon as they could. Back in Goodwell, the Forester children mobilized for the move. They added hoops and tarps, and a hand-built box for storing and serving food, to a 1928 Chevy truck, converting it into a modern-day covered wagon. But Mrs. Forester's aged and blind mother refused to leave, so Slats, who had recovered, was left behind to care for her.

They made their sad good-byes, and brother Clois took the wheel, with his frail mother in the front seat next to him. Then the other seven Forester children scrambled aboard, and they set off for California. "It was pretty exciting for me because it was hope in a hopeless little heart," Louise said.

"We were going to California and would have oranges! And we would have fruit and we would live happily. And so it was just an exciting time. I couldn't wait to get there."

With the mattresses rolled up and stuffed in the truck bed, the children alternated where they sat in the rear. (Louise's favorite spot was right over the wheel of the truck; when the side tarps were rolled up she could survey the countryside they were passing through. She was thrilled one day to see her first weeping willow tree.)

Clois, chosen as the driver, also established himself as the trail boss. "He herded us around," Shirley Forester McKenzie recalled. "He was a Nervous Nellie anyway," Robert Forester said, "and he had lots of tribulations when he had to take this job, because it was a big job. He's a twenty-one-year-old guy and he's taking his sick mother and bunch of kids all the way to California." (He was so intent on his task that once, at a bump in the road when the family dog jostled off the back, the children

THE FORESTERS' EXODUS: Harry Forester's children and wife (saying goodbye to their extended family, opposite, top, and above) and the truck they converted into a 1930s Conestoga wagon to join him in Oakland. Mrs. Forester, in poor health, couldn't persuade her 90-year-old mother (above, right) to leave Oklahoma. At 21, Clois (opposite, left) was put in charge of the move.

had trouble convincing him to pull over so it could be retrieved.) On the other hand, William Forester remembered how many stops Clois seemed to make: "My brother was obsessed with the potential that we might run out of gas. So he stopped at damn near every gas station to top off the tank. It was a little four-banger Chevy, and he drove it about a maximum of thirty-five miles an hour. It took a long time."

They all worried about their mother's fragile health, which prompted them to stop a number of times so she could recoup her strength, especially when a dust storm overtook them in New Mexico. (Clois stopped at an Indian reservation and had her checked out at a Bureau of Indian Affairs clinic.) "She was asthmatic and that was the great problem," according to William Forester:

And she was worn down by the travails of the previous years and by the absence of her husband and by the tragedy of the death of her brother and her sister and leaving her mother. And she was just in bad shape.

She was very feeble all along the way. Instead of camping one night in New Mexico, we used a little of our scarce money to rent a motel so that she could be sleeping out of the dust.

In eastern Arizona, despite her condition, Mrs. Forester insisted that Clois drive through the Painted Desert and the Petrified Forest, which she had always yearned to see. "My mother's health got worse after that," William said, "and we felt that it was necessary to just stop and not travel, so that she could have time being still and resting in a cool, shaded place—Williams, Arizona, in a ponderosa pine forest, at a nice high altitude."

Farther on, they had to descend to the Colorado River on a winding road unlike anything on the southern Plains. "The dreaded Oatman Grade, which is located just outside of Needles," Robert said. "This was a place that struck fear into the hearts of the flatlanders because they had never seen people driving down roads like this. And so lots of stories passed through the people who were on their way, and they all were afraid of the Oatman Grade." Clois kept the truck in low gear for the slow, but successful descent to the Colorado River and the

crossing into California, where they had a rude shock at Needles.

"I had a strong anxiety to see the orange groves," said Shirley, "and it was a great disappointment to come down that grade and to come into California and be down there in the brush and the dryness. Where were these beautiful orange groves? I expected them to be there, hocus-pocus, but they weren't." Louise was even more disappointed. "You're in the desert," she said, "and I just went 'Oh my god, no,' because I was just brokenhearted. I thought there'd be orange groves right there."

West of Needles lay the Mojave Desert, renowned for its fierce heat. Clois decided they should cross it at night. His wisdom was proved by the fact that none of his younger siblings remembered the desert crossing: they were all asleep on the mattresses in back as the truck made the crossing to Barstow. There they turned north, up the Central Valley, and finally made it to Oakland, on the moist San Francisco Bay, where Harry Forester had rented a house and was waiting anxiously for them to arrive. The children's anticipation, no less powerful than their father's, etched the day in their emotional memories.

"We got into Oakland," said Louise, with each turn of the road still mapped in her mind. "And we went to Lake Merritt and went up Grand Avenue and turned right on Moraga and went up Moraga Avenue. We're in the hills now, in the Oakland hills, which are pretty steep for someone like us."

"When we stopped in the canyon and telephoned that we were coming up the road, we were a mile and a half from the house," William said. "We started driving and Dad started hustling. And he raced down to the bottom of the canyon so that he was standing beside the road as we came driving by ten minutes later." Only age five at the time, William had trouble holding back tears recalling the reunion seventy-five years after the fact. So did Louise:

And my dad met us at the corner of Pine Haven Road and Heather Ridge Way, and he had a house rented just up the corner a ways. And I remember sitting in the back of the truck, waiting for my dad to come and greet us, while he was greeting Mom and my brother and whoever had been riding with them.

Then he came around back and started lifting us out one at a time and

ALONG ROUTE 66: The Foresters stopped often at gas stations (top, left), but only used a motel (above) when Mrs. Forester's health deteriorated. Still, she insisted on seeing the Painted Desert and Petrified Forest (top, right). The steep and winding Oatman Grade (opposite, top) brought them to Needles, California. Across the Central Valley, they saw others like them looking for anyplace to stop for the night (opposite, bottom).

SAN FRANCISCO BAY FROM SKY LINE.

giving us a hug and putting us down. And I looked around and I thought, "Oh, yes, we have come to Canaan Land."

Then Harry Forester, who had once dreamed of amassing so much land that he could bestow each of his sons with one square mile of rolling Oklahoma prairie, showed them all their new home: a rented house of three rooms, on a hill so steep the buildings needed stilts to be level.

Instead of the small house, what Robert Forester remembered was the hilly terrain and the pines and eucalyptus trees on them—"sixty, seventy, eighty-feet tall, big trees," he said. "And that was spectacular. It wasn't Oklahoma, you know. 'Toto, we aren't in Oklahoma anymore.'"

For Shirley Forester McKenzie, the important difference was the climate of the Bay Area compared to the Dust Bowl:

Especially to a fair-skinned, freckle-faced, red-headed youngster that I was, that hot wind always just burned me. And this was damp and humid. The fog and the mist were so welcome.

And the mist and the rain were so light, that we kids would go off to school that first year without a hat or a coat or anything because we just loved the feeling of that moisture on us.

We were parched, too.

The hills of Oakland, with San Francisco Bay in the distance.

FORESTERS REUNITED: Harry (back row, third from right) looks satisfied to have his family together in California. Rose, his wife (in striped blouse), still shows signs of worry on her face.

Chapter 9

THOU SHALT NOT BEAR FALSE WITNESS

This is one of the worst sustained environmental disasters in American history. It's not something that happens in just one year; it's not something that just lasts for three or four years; it's a decade.

Because of the combination of extreme drought and extreme high temperatures, this is the worst ten-year period in recorded history on the Plains.

You have ten years of very significant drought; you have some of the highest recorded temperatures on record; you have the winds that were always there; you have soil that was always prone to blowing, but now even more of it than ever had been plowed, had been put into wheat production instead of being used as grazing land.

You get that convergence of factors and you end up with this tremendous disaster.

—Pamela Riney-Kehrberg

IN MARCH 1936, ROBERT GEIGER, the Associated Press reporter who had given the Dust Bowl its name the day after Black Sunday, returned to the area around Boise City. There had been some precipitation over the winter, and farmers were looking forward to a better crop year.

"The Dust Bowl," Geiger wrote, "is losing its handle." But the drought quickly reasserted itself, and 1936 would prove to be virtually as dry as 1935, only with even more dust storms. "The water just didn't soak in," Wayne Lewis said of the few rains that occurred. "I can remember seeing drops of water completely covered with dust rolling on the dust. Now it shouldn't have done that. It was dry and so we didn't create any crops. One of those years, we put our entire wheat crop in one wagon, which is maybe fifty bushels." Texas County, Oklahoma, which in the 1920s had been the top winter wheat–growing county in the nation, harvesting more than 17 bushels of wheat per acre in some years, had dropped to averaging half a bushel per acre.

By now, those who remained in the Dust Bowl had found that one way to deal with what was happening to them was to poke fun at it. "The Panhandle sandstorm will move more dirt in an hour than a hundred realtors can in several days," wrote the *Muleshoe Journal* in northern Texas. "It will turn a chicken's feathers wrong side out quicker than a housewife can pick it for dinner. If it were not for the fact that the wind blows about as much in one direction as another, farmers would frequently have to travel many miles to cultivate the land that was really theirs." A related joke told of a Texas farmer who traveled to Kansas to pay his property taxes, because that's where his farm had ended up. Another said farmers had found a new way to plant their crops: tossing seed in the air as their fields passed overhead.

Boots McCoy liked the story that tried to explain just how hard the wind could blow: "There's an old sayin' that one of the old-timers was tellin' the people, that they had a chain wrapped around a corner post, and he said when that chain got to stickin' out straight, that was a pretty good wind. But when it went to snappin' the chain's links off, it was damned windy."

Crows, another story went, had learned to fly backward, to keep the dust out of

Yet another storm descends on Borger, Texas (top), but as the drought and dust persisted, some residents found that humor helped them endure the troubles (above).

Preceding pages:
Contemplating a barren landscape near Guymon, Oklahoma.

their eyes. And when a pilot, whose engine had stalled because of airborne dirt, bailed out of his airplane, it took him six hours to shovel his way down to earth. A farmer was said to have fainted when a drop of rain hit him on his head; his wife revived him by throwing three buckets of sand in his face.

"There were many jokes about the dust, so that we laughed so we wouldn't cry, I guess," said Pauline Durrett Robertson. "One of them was that a rancher, after a big dust storm, walked out to see about his land. He was trying to find the barbed wire fence that had been covered with dirt. He saw the tops of it, and there was a cowboy's hat. So he walked over and picked up the cowboy's hat—and underneath was the cowboy. And he said, 'Oh my goodness. Aren't you in trouble there? You're covered with dust.' And the cowboy said, 'Well I think I'm gonna be okay, but this horse I'm riding is in a little trouble.' "

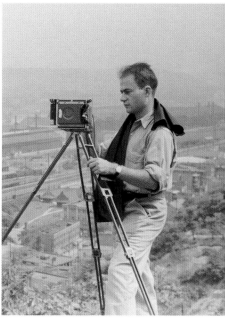

Homesteader Caroline Henderson wrote:

> Since [some] very limited rains . . . gave some slight ground for renewed hope, optimism has been the approved policy. Printed articles or statements by journalists, railroad officials, and secretaries of small-town Chambers of Commerce have heralded too enthusiastically the return of prosperity to the drought region. . . .
>
> But you wished to know the truth, so I am telling you the actual situation.
>
> The longing for rain has become almost an obsession. We remember the gentle all-night rains that used to make a grateful music on the shingles close above our heads, or the showers that came just in time to save a dying crop.
>
> We dream of the faint gurgling sound of dry soil sucking in the grateful moisture of the early or the later rains; of the fresh green of sprouting wheat or barley, the reddish bronze of springing rye. But we waken to another day of wind and dust and hopes deferred. . . .
>
> In telling you of these conditions I realize that I expose myself to charges of disloyalty to this western region. A good Kansas friend suggests that we should imitate the Californian attitude toward earthquakes and keep to ourselves what we know about dust storms.

IN APRIL, ANOTHER OUTSIDER showed up in Boise City. Arthur Rothstein was twenty-one years old, the son of Jewish immigrants, born and raised in New York City. He was in No Man's Land to take photographs for the federal government's Resettlement Administration.

Rothstein's boss, Roy Stryker, believed that pictures could be a powerful tool to show the public not only the multitude of problems the nation was facing, but what the government was doing about them. Over the course of seven years, as the agency became part of the Farm Security Administration (FSA), Stryker would launch an unprecedented documentary effort, eventually amassing more than 200,000 images of America in the 1930s taken by a talented cadre of photographers, including Walker Evans, Russell Lee, Marion Post Walcott, John Vachon, Gordon Parks, and Dorothea Lange.

Sent by the federal government to document the Dust Bowl, Arthur Rothstein (above) met Art Coble and his two sons south of Boise City (above, left, and opposite) struggling to hold onto their farm, buried by sand drifts. As he was saying goodbye, Rothstein captured his most famous photograph (page 156).

"He wanted them to show the things that were wrong, the things that needed to be changed," according to historian Donald Worster. "So they went out with a mission to point out the failures, to point out the poverty, to point out the land problems that the country was facing and to document those. To arouse sympathy among the public who had never been to this part of the country—for the people, yes, but also for the future of the country."

"And he sent them out there with a very simple set of instructions," added Timothy Egan. "He said, 'I want to see their eyes. I want to see their faces. I want to see emotion. I want people to look at these pictures and not see abstraction. I want them to see folks struggling in the land.' "

Arthur Rothstein had been the first photographer Stryker hired—fresh out of Columbia University, idealistic, and so thoroughly a New Yorker that he had to learn how to drive a car in order to take the job. Prior to arriving in Oklahoma, he had documented rural people being dispossessed to create Shenandoah National Park, desperate tenant farmers in Arkansas, hard-luck ranchers in Montana, and slum dwellers in St. Louis. But the most distressing situation he ever encountered, he remembered later, was what he saw driving through the Dust Bowl. "It was like a landscape of the moon," he said, populated by "hardworking people . . . who, through no fault of their own . . . needed assistance. And the only place they could get that assistance was from the government."

About 14 miles south of Boise City, he came across Art Coble, digging out a fence post from a sand drift. Coble and his brother had moved to the area from Illinois during the 1920s wheat boom; the drought had driven the brother back to the Midwest, but Coble was trying to stick it out.

Rothstein chatted with Coble and his two young sons, snapped a few pictures, and was getting back into his car when the wind picked up. Looking back, he saw them bending into the storm, pointed his camera at them, and clicked the shutter.

Rothstein would go on to take hundreds more photographs of drought-stricken farmers, and was so thoroughly dedicated to his task that his camera eye became infected by dust and required an operation, making him a left-eyed photographer

for the rest of his life. But the image Rothstein captured at the Coble farm was soon widely reprinted across the country, touching emotional chords with everyone who saw it, becoming the iconic picture of the Dust Bowl and one of the most widely reproduced photographs of the twentieth century.

"You'd see real people, you'd see real suffering," writer Timothy Egan said. "You'd see someone that you might recognize as folks living down the street. They weren't abstractions anymore. Arthur Rothstein caught drama. He caught storms and humans wrapped up in this thing. And they're extraordinarily powerful. They did help to move public opinion."

"In many respects those photographs were far more important beyond the Dust Bowl than they were in the Dust Bowl," said agricultural historian R. Douglas Hurt. "People who lived here hated them and thought this was a great libel on their way of life, on them, on their country. Some people complained that the government photographers came out and all they did was take pictures of the bad places. They really believed that all of these outsiders made them look bad and by making them look bad questioned their ability and their intelligence: 'Why would you let something like this happen? How can you live here? How can you endure? Don't you have something you can do to improve your livelihood? Why don't you leave?' They took pictures of sand dunes, you know. They didn't show up when the days were good, when you have blue skies and people going about their business normally. They were emphasizing the worst of the region. And what's more, they didn't have that faith in the future. They weren't people that could understand how you could stick and how you could wait for next year."

Reprinted thousands of times, Rothstein's photo of Art Coble and his sons became the nation's visual representation of the Dust Bowl.

By now, the crisis in the Dust Bowl had caught the attention of the major news media of the time—magazines, big-city newspapers, and the newsreel companies that produced short reports shown in movie theaters across the country before the Hollywood films that were the main attraction. The famous photographer Margaret Bourke-White came out and took pictures for prominent magazines like *Fortune* and *Life*. (One of her attempts to photograph the Dust Bowl from the air was thwarted by a storm that grounded her plane.) Ernie Pyle, a roving correspondent and columnist for the Scripps Howard newspaper chain, crisscrossed the southern Plains throughout the summer and filed a number of dispatches, struggling to find the words to describe the devastation he witnessed:

> *The world of drought finally becomes an immersion that levels the senses. You arrive at a point where you no longer look and say, "My God, this is awful!" You gradually become accustomed to dried field and burned pasture; it stretches into a dull, continuous fact.*

Day upon day of driving through this ruined country gradually becomes a sameness that ceases to admit a perspective. You come to accept it as a vast land that is dry and bare, and was that way yesterday and will be tomorrow, and was that way a hundred miles back and will be a hundred miles ahead.

The story is the same everywhere, the farmers say the same thing, the fields look the same—it becomes like the drone of a bee, and after a while you hardly notice it at all.

It was that way all day. It is only at night, when you are alone in the enveloping heat and cannot sleep, and look into the darkness, and things come back to you like a living dream, that you once more realize the stupendousness of it.

Then you can see something more than field after brown field, or a mere succession of dry water holes, or the matter-of-fact resignation on farm faces.

You can see then the whole backward evolution into oblivion of a great land, and the destruction of a people, and the calamity of long years on end without

Two more Rothstein photographs from Boise City in April 1936—"like a landscape of the moon," he remembered.

Farm Security Administration photographs like these of a farmer in Texas (by Dorothea Lange, left) and Kansas (by Russell Lee, above) were meant to humanize the crisis and combat the image some in the East held that the Dust Bowl was populated by "inferior men."

privilege for those of the soil, and the horror of a life started in emptiness, knowing only struggle, and ending in despair.

"If you would like to have your heart broken, just come out here," Pyle told his readers. "It is the saddest land I have ever seen." The iconoclastic essayist, H. L. Mencken, on the other hand, was not as sympathetic, extending his contempt for Roosevelt to those the president was trying to help (and writing from Baltimore, without bothering to set foot on the Plains). "They are simply, by God's inscrutable will, inferior men," Mencken wrote, "and inferior they will remain until, by a stupendous miracle, He gives them equality among His angels."

No one was more sensitive to the image of the southern Plains than John L. McCarty of the *Dalhart Texan*. He and his newspaper had become staunch supporters of Howard Finnell's efforts to teach better farming techniques, as well as many of the New Deal programs, "most of them," he wrote, "honestly and sincerely serving the nation."

But he hated the term "Dust Bowl," fiercely opposed any proposals to encourage outward migration, and was increasingly convinced that Eastern reporters and opinion makers were creating an unfair stereotype of his region and its people. When a reporter for *Collier's* magazine toured the region and wrote a long article entitled "Land Where Our Children Die," portraying the residents as uneducated yokels, McCarty responded with an angry editorial, "Thou Shalt Not Bear False Witness," and offered a paragraph-by-paragraph rebuttal of the story.

McCarty reserved his strongest ire for people from the region he thought contributed to the unfavorable public image. In his mind, they were traitors.

Alexandre Hogue was a painter who had grown up in Texas, and his stark portrayals of the land he thought had been sorely misused began to get national attention, showing up in *Life* magazine, which gave him the title, "the artist of the Dust

Alexandre Hogue's paintings, like *The Last Survivor* (above), infuriated some Texas legislators and boosters, who wanted them destroyed.

Bowl." An angry West Texas Chamber of Commerce denied that Hogue's paintings were works of art, and the Texas House of Representatives voted to censure them.

That wasn't enough for John McCarty. Learning that one of Hogue's paintings was being exhibited at the Pan-American Exposition in Dallas, he and his friends in the Last Man Club swung into action. They took up a collection to buy the painting, with the intention of bringing it back to Dalhart for a very public burning on the city streets. They came back empty-handed. Hogue's painting had sold for $2,000, and McCarty's contingent from Dalhart had been able to raise only $50.

But for McCarty, the worst insult came in the summer of 1936, when a new movie opened at Dalhart's Mission Theater. Directed by Pare Lorentz, with a musical score by the renowned Virgil Thomson, *The Plow That Broke the Plains* had been financed with $20,000 from the

Resettlement Administration as a documentary film meant to describe the causes of the Dust Bowl and how Roosevelt's New Deal was responding to the crisis.

The film placed much of the blame on the arrival of the tractor to the southern Plains, and described how sturdy farmers who had once slowly turned the soil behind a team of mules suddenly became a mechanized force arrayed against nature itself. It had been shot partly in the Dalhart region, and the person seen most often on-screen—though he had no speaking role—was Bam White, the half-Apache local ex-cowboy who, like many cattlemen, had always harbored private doubts about the wisdom of turning so much of the grasslands into wheat fields.

White had been chosen by the film's director not because of his opinions, but simply because he still had an old plow and a horse to pull it. He was paid $25 for two hours' work in front of the cameras—more than he had ever made in such a short time, and a windfall for his impoverished family of five. White had never even been to a movie until he attended the Dalhart premiere of *The Plow That Broke the Plains* and saw himself on the big screen. The local reaction, however, was largely negative. "They didn't like seeing their land or themselves as characters on the bad end of a drama," Egan said. A Texas delegate to the Democratic convention that year demanded that it not be shown at the convention and that the president and his government withdraw it from public viewing in movie theaters. He even threatened to punch the director of the Resettlement Administration in the nose for having the film made in the first place.

But the film had already been previewed by the president and members of Congress in Washington, and was showing in New York and other major cities around the nation, alongside popular movies like Charlie Chaplin's *Modern Times* and *Poor Little Rich Girl*, starring Shirley Temple. All that attention, an incensed John McCarty editorialized, "is bound to do more damage to our credit and our agriculture than it can possibly do good." On the streets of Dalhart, Bam White found himself shunned, called a half-breed and a turncoat.

When more and more newsreel companies began showing up to make their own short films, McCarty reached his limit:

The High Plains region is a helpless underdog . . . experiencing a vicious libel about which it can do nothing, because the libel has already been perpetuated—like a slanderous false whisper about a pure girl, like the rumor that starts a run on the bank, or the . . . old myth about the "Great American Desert."

Take your movie cameras, your magazines, radios, and newspapers, and go to hell with them. . . . All we ask of you now is to be let alone.

Pare Lorentz's feature-length documentary, *The Plow That Broke the Plains* (below, left), was also financed by FDR's New Deal, as were the 200,000 Farm Security Administration images captured by photographers like Arthur Rothstein (a plow near Boise City, below) and Dorothea Lange (a girl in a sod house in New Mexico, opposite).

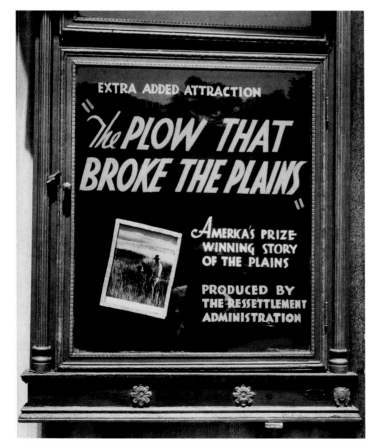

By plowing deeper furrows (above) and doing it on the contour of the land (top, left), farmers following Howard Finnell's methods were slowly beginning to hold the soil in place (top, right).

Not everyone in the Dust Bowl felt so slighted. "Sometimes at the movies the newsreel showed the Dust Bowl, and that infuriated the local boosters," Pauline Durrett Robertson remembered, "because they said, 'That's bad publicity. We don't need that bad publicity! And they should not tell that about us to the world. We're more than the dust storms.' The rest of us thought, 'Well, they got that right. They're really telling what's happening to us. They're really telling it right.'"

The Kingdom of Nature is not a democracy; we cannot repeal natural laws when they become irksome. We have got to learn to conform to those laws or suffer severer consequences than we have already brought upon ourselves.

We Americans have been the greatest destroyers of land of any race or people, barbaric or civilized.

Unless immediate steps are taken to restore grass to millions of these sun-scorched, wind-eroded lands, we shall have on our hands a new, man-made Sahara where formerly was rich grazing land.

History has shown time and time again that no large nation can long endure the continuous mismanagement of its soil resources. The world is strewn with the ruins of once flourishing civilizations, destroyed by erosion.

—*Hugh Hammond Bennett*

IN AUGUST, DALHART HAD ANOTHER visitor: Hugh Hammond Bennett, the head of the Soil Conservation Service. He was traveling from Amarillo, Texas, to the Dakotas, with a committee of experts expected to make a report to President Roosevelt about conditions on the Great Plains. (Arthur Rothstein was along to take photographs of the committee's tour.) Their first stop was Dalhart, to meet with his soil scientist, Howard Finnell, who showed Bennett the progress on "Operation Dust Bowl."

Bulldozers and heavy machinery were tearing at the big dunes north of town, and reseeding them with Sudan grass and other plants to hold the soil in place. Besides attacking the Dalhart dunes, Finnell had set up thirteen other demonstration projects in his vast region, manned by CCC enrollees and WPA workers.

He had sent photographers up in airplanes to take aerial photographs of the land, and used the pictures along with soil samples taken on the ground to decide which parcels had the best chance to grow wheat and other crops again and which should be restored to grassland.

"Finnell understood that farmers had to see the proof," historian R. Douglas Hurt said. "And many of them were skeptical that much of what the Soil Conservation Service was trying to get them to do wouldn't work, given the environmental conditions of the time. And so why put the money and the effort into it if you were gonna fail anyway? But Finnell was an optimist in many respects. He really did believe that if you did certain things, this land would be as productive as it had been in the past, and the future was very bright. But certain sensible things had to be done. It took convincing, and it took demonstration—and in some respects it took payment of farmers to get them on board."

Slowly, Finnell was making headway with the farmers he was trying to convert. Earlier in the year, he had petitioned Secretary of Agriculture Henry Wallace for $2 million in emergency funds to offer incentives of 20 cents an acre for those who would try his method of contour listing on their own land. Nearly 40,000 farmers had signed up and gone to work on 5.5 million acres.

"The only program that was out there that was effective was this one," according to Donald Worster. "There was nothing else that the government really was able to do except the Soil Conservation Service's

The renowned photographer Margaret Bourke-White captured both intimate portraits and aerial photographs (below right and bottom) of the Dust Bowl for national magazines. Hugh Bennett wanted a closer, personal inspection of the soils with Howard Finnell (below).

initiatives. And Finnell was the point man to try to make it work among these farmers who had still not admitted that it was their fault, farmers who basically said, 'This is all nature's doing. Leave us alone. The rains will come back and we will be back in business.'"

After Dalhart, Bennett and his committee went to Boise City, and then moved on with their tour of the Plains, wending their way north through Colorado, Kansas, Nebraska, South Dakota, Wyoming, and North Dakota. In Bismarck they met up with President Roosevelt, who was on his own 4,000-mile whistle-stop tour across the Midwest and northern Plains, and gave him their report.

Entitled *The Future of the Great Plains*, it estimated that 80 percent of the region was in some stage of erosion, and pointed to what it called "the basic cause" of the problem—"an attempt," it said, "to impose upon the region a system of agriculture to which the Plains are not adapted." Too much land had been plowed up, Bennett said, and too much of it was converted to a single crop—wheat—using the wrong methods of farming. But, it concluded, the nation "cannot afford to let the farmer fail.

We endanger our democracy, if we allow the Great Plains, or any other section of the country, to become an economic desert."

Roosevelt was not about to let that happen, as he made abundantly clear to the crowd at the Bismarck train station: "Back East, there have been all kinds of reports that out in the drought area there was despondency, a lack of hope for the future, and a general atmosphere of gloom. But I had a hunch—and it was the right one—that when I got out here I would find that you people had your chins out, that you were not looking forward to the day when this country would be depopulated, but that you and your children expect to remain here." Two weeks later, in one of his famous fireside chats, the President elaborated more fully for a national radio audience:

My friends, I have been on a journey of husbandry. . . . I talked with families who had lost their wheat crop, lost their corn crops, lost their livestock, lost the water in their well, lost their garden and come through the end of the summer without one dollar of cash resources, facing a winter without

While Hugh Bennett toured the southern Plains (speaking to farmers in Springfield, Colorado, above, left), President Roosevelt headed to the Dakotas by train (above) and then talked with farmers there (opposite, top).

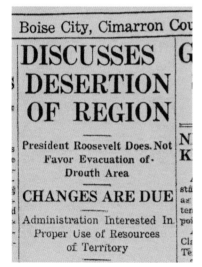

Boise City, Cimarron Cou[

DISCUSSES DESERTION OF REGION

President Roosevelt Does Not Favor Evacuation of Drouth Area

CHANGES ARE DUE

Administration Interested In Proper Use of Resources of Territory

Roosevelt's decision against encouraging the depopulation of the Dust Bowl—and instead to do everything possible to help farmers stay on the land—made the front page of the *Boise City News* (above).

feed or food—facing a planting season without seed to put in the ground.

I shall never forget the fields of wheat so blasted by heat that they cannot be harvested. . . . I saw brown pastures which would not keep a cow on fifty acres. Yet I would not have you think for a single minute that there is permanent disaster in these drought regions, or that the picture I saw meant depopulating these areas.

No cracked earth, no blistering sun, no burning wind . . . are a permanent match for the indomitable American farmers and stockmen and their wives and children who have carried on through desperate days, and inspire us with their self-reliance, their tenacity, and their courage.

It was their fathers' task to make homes; it is their task to keep those homes; it is our task to help them with their fight.

"Here's a land that God himself seems to have given up on, getting the backhand of nature," said Timothy Egan. "So nature, God, whatever you wanted to call it, had itself deserted this land. And the fact that the president still gave it his attention—somebody looked at this area as something other than godforsaken leftover—that was a very big deal at a time when they felt so abandoned."

"To us he was a savior," said Virginia Kerns Frantz. "He just gave us hope where we had none. And I can remember my dad saying that he normally didn't vote Democrat but he thought he would that time. And I think he became a staunch Democrat after that."

Chapter 10

OKIES

There is a strange new population of 250,000 in California, and this number grows at the appalling rate of something like 100 a day. These are the migratory farm workers.

The majority of them are dispossessed families from Oklahoma, Kansas, Nebraska, Arkansas, Texas, and other Midwest states. . . .

These people have migrated halfway across America in the simple and honorable search for work and food and shelter. They even dream of owning a little farm, a small rich piece of magic California earth.

Under existing conditions, this last must surely be a dream. The small, independent farmer is almost extinct in these western valleys, which are controlled by . . . big growers, absentee corporation owners, and banks.

Wherever they settle for a little while in trailer, tent, abandoned barn or shed, they are ostracized, they live apart: they are migrants and Okies.

—*Sanora Babb*

DURING THE DECADE OF THE Great Depression, California's population would grow more than 20 percent, an increase of 1.3 million people. More than half of the newcomers came from cities, not farms; one in six were professionals or white-collar workers. Of the 315,000 who arrived from Oklahoma, Texas, and neighboring states, only 16,000 were from the Dust Bowl itself.

But regardless of where they actually came from, regardless of their skills and their education and their individual reasons for seeking a new life in a new place, to most Californians—and to the nation at large—they were all the same.

And they all had the same name: Okies. "We were made fun of," said Louise Forester Briggs. "You know, 'Talk some more; you talk funny.' And you hated that because it set you apart."

For many of them, the discrimination was far worse than having their accents ridiculed. "There was a sign in a movie theater in the Central Valley of California which basically said, NIGGERS AND OKIES UPSTAIRS," said historian Donald Worster.

"That is, you can't sit down here with 'real people'; the Okies are 'white trash.' " In some instances, the treatment mirrored that of African Americans in the all-white "sundown towns" of the southern Plains from which they came, according to

Preceding pages:
A photo from the "Migrant Mother" series shot by Dorothea Lange.

The "Okies" who tried to find work in the agricultural fields of California's Central Valley (below) often ended up living in squalid camps (opposite, top) or along the roadside (opposite, bottom).

Timothy Egan: "There were signs similar to the signs they had in Dalhart, Texas, that said, Black man don't let the sun go down on you here. Similarly, there were signs all throughout the Central Valley saying, Okie, go back. We don't want you."

About a third of all the recent arrivals—many of them former sharecroppers from the Cotton Belt—ended up in California's agricultural valleys, where the farms had always relied on migrant labor (Mexicans, Filipinos, Asians) to pick their cotton, vegetables, and fruit. They settled in developments called "Little Oklahomas" and "Okievilles," or moved with the harvests, sometimes traveling seven hundred to a thousand miles in the season, staying in squalid roadside camps called "jungles" or simply putting up a tent along the road

or in an unused field. And they found themselves at the mercy of the growers—and the contractors who drummed up the fieldworkers each day.

Sanora Babb, who had returned to California and taken a job with the Farm Security Administration (FSA), and was trying to help the newly arrived migrants, explained how the exploitation worked:

> [The] labor contractor drives through the country, stopping at farms, makes estimates of the amount of cotton, and makes an offer to the grower to pick it for so much.
>
> Then he drives along the camps, talks to the "Okies," and tells them all to go to a certain farm where several hundred men are needed, at good wages (perhaps at 80 cents). Then he drives to another camp and repeats the offer. . . .
>
> Finally, where three hundred men are actually needed, one thousand or two thousand and five hundred will appear. The offered price at once comes down, and most of them leave without work. They have arrived with their last bit of gas and no food at "home" so that they are forced to take anything.

With her boss Tom Collins, the energetic and idealistic FSA administrator for the region, Sanora went up and down the Central Valley, informing the newcomers about programs to provide them with food and medical assistance for their families, education for their children, and better living conditions. On weekends, Sanora's sister Dorothy, a gifted amateur photographer, often joined them and took pictures.

Through photographs, Sanora Babb's sister, Dorothy, chronicled the human suffering of the "Okies" (opposite and above) that Sanora was recording in her journals. Her work was overshadowed by the FSA photographs of Dorothea Lange (above, right).

When the refugees learned that the Babb sisters had grown up on the southern Plains, it helped establish a trust and respect that extended both ways. "They have the simple and sturdy values often bemoaned as lost," Sanora noted. "They are a proud, strong people, patient, uncomplaining, intelligent. They want first of all to work, to have a home for their families, to educate their children, to put something by for the future. These simple rights are part of the heritage of Americans; it is difficult for them to understand that none of them remain. Their whole lives are concentrated now on one instinctive problem, that of keeping alive."

Sanora did her best to record the abject conditions she and Collins were encountering every day:

> *I saw many families who had had no work, and were too weak and hungry to look for any more. Some of them had no beds and were sleeping in old barns on hay or on the bare ground. One pregnant woman with nine children was sleeping in a shed with several calves in order to keep warm.*
>
> *Only a few days ago we met a young man walking along the road to town in search of immediate work and help. His wife had had a baby three days before in an abandoned milk house separated from any camp, where they had taken refuge during the recent storms.*
>
> *He was desperate. Since the birth, his wife, their other children, and he himself had not eaten for three days. If he did not get something for them at once, she and the baby would die.*

The FSA had also asked the photographer Dorothea Lange to document the deplorable conditions among the migrants. Tom Collins used her photos to push for

MIGRANT MOTHER: Dorothea Lange (top) came across Florence Thompson and her children in a pea pickers' camp in Nipomo, California, in March 1936 (see photo, pages 166–167). Thompson, from eastern Oklahoma, had moved to California in 1925, long before the Dust Bowl. Her husband had died in 1931, leaving her with five children, whom she tried to support by moving with the harvests. Lange took a series of photos (including the previously unpublished one above), but the one at left became what Roy Stryker called "the ultimate photo of the Depression Era" and was used by the FSA to press for better programs for the migrant workers.

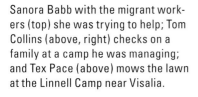

Sanora Babb with the migrant workers (top) she was trying to help; Tom Collins (above, right) checks on a family at a camp he was managing; and Tex Pace (above) mows the lawn at the Linnell Camp near Visalia.

creation of government-run camps with better shelter and sanitation for the steady stream of refugees, who were arriving every day. Collins insisted that the camps be self-governed, with elected committees responsible for everything from sewing clubs and libraries to child care and cleanliness. But only a lucky few were able to find space there.

Fresh from the Texas Panhandle, Tex Pace and his parents ended up at the Linnell camp near Visalia. "They loved it," he said.

"You had a big building in the middle of the cabins with a shower. You had washing machines, you had clotheslines and ironing rooms. It was much better than living on a ditch bank."

While the growers depended on the migrants for cheap labor, the townspeople didn't appreciate anything—like the government camps—that encouraged them to stay. Nor did the growers once the harvest was over. "When the work was done, they didn't need 'em," Tex said. "So the camps had a lot of opposition. They wouldn't win a popularity contest."

One of Tex's duties was editing the camp newspaper, while he also tried to advance his education at a community college, where he was made to feel unwelcome. "I lived in the camp," he said. "I didn't make it a secret where I was from. I was goin' to school to try to better myself. So what they thought of me didn't matter. They made remarks about Okies that you always heard all the time. But I think you make your name yourself."

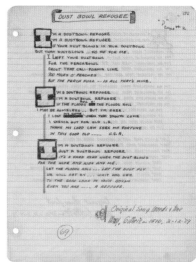

We'd always been taught to believe that these 48 states was an absolutely free country. And that anytime anybody took a notion to get up, and go anywhere in these 48 states, that nobody else . . . would proceed to ask him a whole bunch of questions or to try to keep him from going where he started out to go.

As I rambled around over the country and kept lookin' at all these people, seein' how they lived outside like coyotes around in the trees an' timber and under the bridges and along all the railroad tracks and in their little shack houses that they built out of cardboard . . . and old corrugated iron that they got out of the dumps—that just struck me to write this song ("I Ain't Got No Home").

—*Woody Guthrie*

LIKE MOST OF THE NEW ARRIVALS, Woody Guthrie had settled in one of California's cities: Los Angeles, where he worked washing dishes and singing in

bars before finally landing his own show on radio station KFVD. Each day he performed his own songs as well as older folk tunes he had learned in Oklahoma and Texas, which reminded many listeners in his growing audience of the homes they had left.

But though he was becoming a well-known radio personality, he, too, felt the sting of bigotry aimed at anyone considered an "Okie." He began spending time traveling and performing for free in the Central Valley, where the treatment of the farmworkers politicized him—and his music—for the rest of his life. He sang at picket lines of workers holding out for a higher wage, and started a newspaper column, *Woody Sez*, in the left-leaning *People's World*. "I ain't a communist necessarily," he said, "but I've been in the red all my life."

Guthrie was offended that the California state legislature nearly passed a law closing the state's borders to people it called "paupers and persons likely to become public charges." Then, without any legal authority, the Los Angeles police chief unilaterally dispatched 125 of his officers to the main

Woody Guthrie (top, left, at the microphone with Cisco Houston) performs for a crowd; the lyrics to his "Dust Bowl Refugee" and his Victor record of "Dusty Old Dust" (above).

Sam Beck (above) in his fifties, a little stooped from his hard life; Harry and Rose Forester (couple at right, above, right) after their move to California; and Harry at age 92 with his children (right) in 1976.

entry points from Arizona, Nevada, and Oregon. For six weeks they intimidated anyone they considered "vagrants"— including Clarence and Irene Beck's father, Sam, from Wheeless, Oklahoma.

"My father was a Dust Bowl Okie," Clarence said. "He got put in jail when he crossed into California because he didn't have fifty bucks. He was arrested as a vagrant." Luckily, an ex-neighbor from Oklahoma knew Sam was coming and arranged to free him by saying he had a place to stay.

For a while, Sam was allowed to live at a chicken farm, where he worked in exchange for eggs to eat. Then he finally landed a job with the Los Angeles highway department and started a new life for himself and his motherless daughter. "A fresh start, I guess that's the words to use," Irene said. "So thank God for that. I was blessed that way."

Sam Beck died of a heart attack in 1947, at age fifty-four, spreading blacktop on a California highway. His travails served as the principal life lesson for his son, Clarence, who got a college education, became a nuclear engineer, and lived to the ripe age of ninety, always remembering what happened to his father:

> He had a tough life. Very tough life. He and his life were the reason that I said, "God, what do I have to do to have money, not be a farmer, and I'll do it. I don't care whether it be a pimp; I don't care whether it's stealing. Whatever it takes, I'm not gonna farm and I'm not going to be broke."
>
> And that's been my driving force. And I'm not a farmer and I'm not broke. I'm not a pimp either, thank God.

Up in Oakland, Harry Forester needed the government's help to support his family—commodities from the relief agencies, temporary jobs with the WPA—until he found more permanent work digging trenches for sewage systems. "I think he just had to keep on putting one foot in front of the other," said his son William. "When he found work he would take it, and when he had to accept relief he would do that as a matter of necessity. But he worked hard. And he was tired in the evening. He was a very pious man. He was the son of a very pious man. And I think he must have had some feelings that God had it in for him, or for the whole country at that time. But it was just a sense of absolute futility on his part."

Although they never inherited a section of land from their father, Harry Forester's sons eventually went to college and on to successful careers, but they would never forget the stigma they felt growing up as "Okies." "That was difficult to deal with because that branded you as a poor boy; that was not easy for me," said Robert Forester. Still, William Forester said, it was nothing compared with how their father felt:

He was a renter until he died. And that flew in the face of his ideal and his dream.

He would say, "Well, I reckon I'll die a pauper." He didn't feel terribly optimistic about his chances of living out the dream that he once harbored when he was a young man.

Calvin Crabill's father, John, had rescued his wife from the dust of eastern Colorado, but the hard times followed him to southern California. "Couldn't get a job, he wouldn't be hired," Calvin said. "Or if he was hired, then he'd be fired soon. And we went on relief. My second sister was born and she was just a little thing. My mother had no milk. So the relief people gave us a quart of milk a day for the baby, but no milk for the rest of us. And I had a little sister who was only two years older and no milk for her, just for the baby. So it was pretty rough."

Calvin was determined to get an education for himself, but his family counted on him to make money for them all to survive:

I was a paperboy for four years, and then at the end of my junior year I got

Calvin Crabill ready to deliver newspapers (below, left) to help support his family; and with his father, mother, and younger siblings (below) during his senior year in high school.

Dorothy Babb took these photographs of the "Okies" her sister was so devoted to. "How brave they all are," Sanora said. "They will endure."

a job at a restaurant. *I worked seventy hours a week that first summer, and my first pay was ten cents an hour for a seventy-hour week.*

My senior year in high school I worked forty hours a week, three nights a week till one o'clock in the morning. And I fell asleep in class the next day. In this one Shakespeare class, I remember the teacher asked me a question, and my head was on my desk. She called my name, and I couldn't answer. She came over and stood over me and called my name. I could hear her calling. I felt like the fighter who is down for the count and can't get up. She called my name again, and she finally said, "Oh, let the poor boy sleep."

[Later] she said, "I'm gonna tell your boss. You're only sixteen. You shouldn't be working after ten o'clock at night."

I said, "If you do, I'll have to quit, and my family needs the money. I have to do it." So she let me do it.

Meanwhile, John Crabill moved from one temporary job to another, a Colorado cowboy far from the Plains he loved. "My father was called an Okie," Calvin said. "He was a gentle, quiet man. So I think he could take it pretty well. It made me with a chip on my shoulder that I probably carry to this day, that I was very aware that I thought I was the poorest kid in high school. We rented a little house on the alley in Burbank. And the house in front, the people had more money. And they were very aware that we were the poor people on the block. In those days you could get something to put on your license plate that would be some kind of a slogan. Well ours said 'Peaceful Valley' [from Colorado]. My father liked that place so he put it on his license plate. Well, he got a job, and the people at his job crossed out the 'V' and wrote 'Peaceful Alley' because they knew he lived on an alley. So if you're down they push you down, fella, they push you down. And that's what happened to him over and over and over, over and over."

How brave they all are. . . . They aren't broken and docile but they don't complain. . . . They all want work and hate to have help.

One day I visited sixty-five families, interviewed thirty men, and walked miles, and came back feeling wonderful. Another day I walked 12 miles seeing people, and felt good . . . tired but pleasantly so. . . .

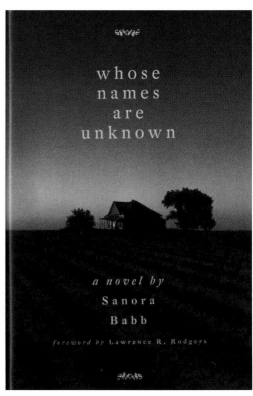

The success of John Steinbeck's novel *The Grapes of Wrath* (above, left) meant Sanora Babb's Dust Bowl novel *Whose Names Are Unknown* (above) would not be published until 2004.

At the end of [another] day, after seeing the people living worse than I had even imagined, I suddenly started to cry while I was eating and had to come back to my room. Once during the day I almost broke, but I had to hold myself tight against it, because they have enough troubles without that, and if we felt bad, they'd feel worse.

—*Sanora Babb*

DURING HER TIME LIVING AND working amongst the migrants, Sanora Babb kept a nightly journal, which she planned to turn into a novel about the Dust Bowl refugees she had met and what they had gone through. She also wrote detailed reports for her boss, Tom Collins, who was regularly sharing her notes with a writer working on a muckraking article for the *San Francisco News*—a published author named John Steinbeck. ("When Steinbeck first came" to the migrant camps, Sanora noted in a letter to her sister, "he had to stop seeing them before the day was out. Tom Collins said he said: 'By God! I can't stand anymore! I'm going away and blow the lid off this place.'")

Sanora Babb herself would eventually send some chapters of her novel to Bennett Cerf, a prominent editor of Random House in New York City, who was so impressed he asked her to come East to talk about it. But by the time she arrived, in the winter of 1939, Steinbeck had come out with his own Pulitzer Prize–winning novel, *The Grapes of Wrath*, which chronicled the tribulations of the Joad family, tenant farmers who had migrated to California from the cotton fields of eastern Oklahoma, not the Dust Bowl. Steinbeck's book was dedicated to Tom Collins and was an immediate best-seller—such a hit, Cerf and other New York editors told Babb, that the market couldn't support a second novel on the same subject. They advised her to put the manuscript aside, which she did and then went on to write other books. Her Dust Bowl novel, *Whose Names Are Unknown*, was finally published in 2004, a year before her death, still fired by the passions aroused in her by the treatment of her fellow "next year" people:

Tex Pace met the girl of his dreams, Dorothy Stephenson, at the Linnell government camp (above). After they were married and Pace went to work at the Santa Maria camp (above, right), they lived in a trailer the officials said John Steinbeck had used during his research of migrant conditions.

You, who live in any kind of comfort or convenience, do not know how these people can survive these things, do you? They will endure because there is no immediate escape from endurance. . . .

But, of course, there's a limit to starvation, a limit to pain, a limit to endurance, patience, struggle.

Some will die. The rest must live.

AT THE LINNELL GOVERNMENT labor camp near Visalia, one night Tex Pace walked in to the talent show that was held each week to entertain the migrant workers and keep their spirits up. That particular evening, a girl named Dorothy Stephenson from Henryetta, Oklahoma, was singing. When she wasn't attending high school, she picked peas and cotton to help support her parents and four siblings.

For Tex, it was love at first sight. "It was the first talent show I'd been to," he said. "I walked in and there she was singin'. I thought, 'By gosh, where I've been all this time?'"

A year later, they were in town, standing in line to get a marriage license, when someone from the Visalia Merchants Association pulled them aside with an offer. As a publicity stunt to promote downtown businesses, the merchants wanted to arrange a wedding on the stage of the Fox Theater, during the intermission of the movie, *The Man I Married.*

If Dorothy and Tex would agree to be that couple, the merchants would buy her a $100 wedding dress and pay for the cake, the bridesmaids' gowns, and other accessories. Each of the wedding guests, however, would still need to buy a movie ticket to attend.

"Nice wedding," Tex remembered, including it in the larger memory of his migration to California. "I met the greatest girl that ever came out of Oklahoma and married her. And she's given me two great sons."

Chapter 11

THE CRUEL CRISIS

April 6, 1937.

After another dry summer in 1936, with only the scantiest production, hope was revived by light rains in late September. This moisture was barely sufficient to encourage the sowing of wheat for the possibility of spring pasturage. . . .

The seed sprouted, but again the hope of a crop has vanished with the dry winter and the raging winds of spring.

The worst storm thus far in 1937 occurred immediately after a slight snowfall which again roused delusive hopes. That snow melted on a Tuesday. Wednesday morning, with a rising wind, the dust began to move again, and until late Friday night there was little respite.

We need no calendar to tell us that planting time is here again. . . . Yet any attempt to proceed with planting under present conditions would be stubborn and expensive folly.

We are now reluctantly feeding [our livestock] the last small remainder of the crop of 1931.

—Caroline Henderson

FOR CAROLINE HENDERSON AND everyone else back in the heart of the Dust Bowl, 1937 would prove to be the worst year yet. Guymon, Oklahoma, just 30 miles southeast of her homestead, was engulfed by six bad dust storms in January, fourteen in February, and then thirteen more in March, including one that closed the schools in nearby Boise City and tore roofs off of buildings a hundred miles away in Dodge City, Kansas.

On Easter morning, Caroline discovered a jackrabbit cowering in the kindling pile near her kitchen door. "He was, however, no frolicsome Easter bunny," she wrote, "but a starved, trembling creature with one eye battered out by the terrific dust storm of the preceding week. He made no effort to escape. I bathed his eye and put him into shelter with our guinea pig, hoping that he would live until showers might bring some tinge of green upon our dust-covered wasteland. Another blinded rabbit picked up in the yard had just died in spite of all my care."

The rabbits and their fates seemed, she thought, like omens: "When these wild creatures, ordinarily so well able to take care of themselves, come seeking protection, their necessity indicates a cruel crisis for man and beast."

The "cruel crisis" was far from over. The storms kept coming. On the afternoon of May 21, 15 miles northwest of the Hendersons, a local photographer named Francis Craver noticed a dust cloud appearing over the Doric Theater in downtown Elkhart, Kansas. He grabbed his camera and chronicled the storm's descent—which caused the high school to cancel commencement ceremonies planned for that evening.

Two weeks later, 50 miles east of the Hendersons, in Hooker, Oklahoma, a furniture salesman named George Risen saw another wall of dirt approaching. He scrambled to the top of the tallest building in town and began taking a remarkable sequence of pictures with his Brownie camera. As it passed, the storm dropped

Caroline Henderson comforts her dog (top, left) while husband Will displays a fossilized fern he found on the windswept fields (top, right); their calves (above) find water in the stock tank supplied by their windmill and well.

Preceding pages:
Deep furrows and contour plowing hold the soil (in foreground), but the field in back is still a wasteland.

3 feet of dust on Hooker and the surrounding area—so much, that the Santa Fe Railway needed snowplows and shovel crews to clear its tracks.

By the end of July, the number of destructive storms would rise to 79; by the end of the year, to 134. And the storms now seemed to last longer—a cumulative total of 550 hours in Guymon. The only difference between the southern Plains and the Sahara desert, one resident suggested, was that a lot of "damned fools" weren't trying to farm the Sahara. Those who tried were averaging only 2 bushels of wheat per acre.

"We'd just keep thinkin' the rains would come," Boots McCoy said. "Everybody said, 'We'll be all right, the rains will come.' Well you know, they didn't come, and we'd just have one storm right after another." (The agricultural extension agents in Dodge City counted the number of dirt storms over the decade, according to historian Pamela Riney-Kehrberg, "and the tally for the 1930s was 726, which is two years spent in the dust,

which means that your troubles just kept coming back and coming back and coming back.")

In Dalhart, Texas, Judge Wilson Cowan presided over "dust lunacy trials," involving farmwives who had snapped from the relentless storms and the social disruption they were causing. "The dust is killing me," one of them cried out as the judge weighed whether to commit her to an asylum. "It's killing my children, it's killing us all. God help us."

"People were having a very hard time knowing who or what to blame for the situation they're in," Riney-Kehrberg said. "Have they done something wrong? There were at least a few people who I talked to about their experiences in the 1930s who said that sometimes they felt like they were being punished. That maybe God was punishing them for having been wasteful, for not having been good stewards of the bounty that He had provided them." Pauline Durrett Robertson remembered church sermons in which the pastor said, "God was mad at us."

DUST STORM - ELKHART, KS. 5-21-

Three of Francis Craver's eight photographs taken on Main Street of Elkhart, Kansas, documenting the black blizzard of May 21, 1937. Floyd Coen remembered the storm—and the man in photo number 1 (top, left) as Mr. Studebaker. Another resident, Della Wray Blythe, wrote: "Even these pictures cannot describe the feeling of doom that we felt on that day."

From the roof of a two-story building in the town center, amateur photographer George Risen took seven pictures of a monstrous storm that swept into Hooker, Oklahoma, on June 4, 1937. For some, the approach of a storm was as frightening as when it hit.

Some churches had trouble staying open. The exodus to other states depleted their congregations. Of those members who stayed, some were ashamed to attend services because they could no longer afford nice clothes, and the economic crisis meant emptier collection plates. Ministers joined the list of other professions having difficulty being paid for their work.

Although the overall populations of Kansas and Oklahoma fell during the 1930s, church membership went up, especially among Pentecostals, Assemblies of God, and Nazarenes. The residents of Elkhart held a mass prayer meeting on Main Street, and asked local businesses to close during it. From the town of Hodgeman, members of a prayer group petitioned President Roosevelt for a thirty-day national prayer vigil so that, they said, "God may come to our rescue speedily."

"The people that was real religious said that God was tryin' to drive us off of the land," Boots McCoy said. "I never did believe that—or Dad never did believe it, and we believed whatever Dad believed, as kids. He said there will just be times that will be bad and times that they won't." Lorene Delay White's father kept promising her that "it will get better and the rains would come again. But I didn't even think about there being an end. It seemed as though this was the way we were going to have to live."

As she went from farm to farm, carrying out her duties as a social worker for the FERA, Dorothy Christenson Williamson was struck equally by the deep despair and the steely resilience she encountered:

> If you were a farmer, you plowed the ground and you put seed in it and it grew up. That was farming. But you didn't expect this dirt that was giving you this food to turn on you like that and destroy you like it did.

A farmer scans the sky for any sign of rain (above, left), while an article in the *Boise City News* asks businesses to close at noon each day for a thirty-minute moment of prayer.

A church in Clayton, New Mexico, about to be covered in dust in May 1937 (above); and a lonely church on the prairie, with a slight haze in the sky (right).

ND.-7515.

It's very difficult to describe. Not only the dust blowing, but the effect it had on you. These poor people didn't have any hope that things would be better. And yet I think to be a dry land farmer you have to be a certain kind of a person. And deep down inside of themselves they must have had the feeling, "If we just stick it out and stay here, times are bound to get better," which did give them a little hope. But in the middle of a dust storm, it's very difficult to hope.

And it takes a lot of willpower and everything else to bring yourself back out time after time after time. So you had to admire those people who did stick it out. They had come there, maybe they'd been born there. And they intended to stay. This was their home.

Though he was grateful to have left farming and the Dust Bowl, and happy to be pointed toward a different future, Clarence Beck fondly remembered those who stayed. "They were good people," he said. "There was nothing about the population that was bad. Everybody was hardworking, trying to make an honest living. And nature just wouldn't let 'em do it. So there were failures and there were also people that were awful hard to knock off of the bush. Ended up that a Depression and the Dust Bowl didn't get 'em all. It left quite a few. It left the hardy ones."

To get by, Virginia Kerns Frantz's parents leaned on each other—and on something more, she said: "Their faith. Both of my parents were very, very good Christians. And no matter what came along, they seemed to accept it. They both just seemed like they were just going on, doing the best they could, and they didn't do a whole lot of griping about it." Around the house, her mother often sang hymns to take her children's minds off the troubles staring them in the face.

Floyd Coen's father tried to convince his family that conditions were actually worse in other parts of the country. "I remember we had the radio and he's listenin' to it talkin' about a flood on the Ohio River and houses floatin' down and people on those houses," Floyd said. "And my dad turned to us and said, 'We've got it better here than they have up there.' And that was in '37. So he thought that the dirt was better than that water."

From her father, trying to hold onto his farm while his wife and youngest children were in Arkansas, Dorothy Sturdivan Kleffman learned that another element of survival was being willing to help others: "If a man became ill, the neighbor men went in and they cut his crop first before their own so that that lady and her children would have some kind of income or help. And then after they did his field, they would go home and take care of their own."

Getting together became important, regardless of the place or circumstance. According to Trixie Travis Brown, after church on Sundays the people of Follett, Texas, often drove out to a designated spot

TOT DIES AT PLAY

Fall In Loose Sand Proves Fatal To Young Son of Felt Couple

An unusual and tragic death occurred in the Felt community last Thursday when Alton Lee, three-year old son of Mr. and Mrs. Glen Jacobs, died suddenly from the effects of having fallen in and breathed a large quantity of dust.

The child was playing about a fresno which was being used by an older brother, Henry, 14 years of age, to clear drifted sand away from the barn at the farm home. He was running along with the horse-drawn implement and tripping, fell into the loose dirt. It is thought a deep breath drew such a large amount of the dust into his throat that his breathing was stopped entirely.

Funeral services were conducted Saturday by Dr. T. F. Rudisill at the Bertrand church and interment followed in the Bertrand cemetery under the direction of Wilder Funeral home.

In the midst of continuing despair and tragedies, like the freak accident reported by the *Boise City News* (above), Virginia Kerns Frantz (holding a Bible and friend, top left) and her family relied on their faith. A storm in Hooker, Oklahoma (opposite), engulfs the town and its Methodist Church.

and "we'd park in a circle around this pit. It was an absolutely barren, treeless, empty lot just outside of town. And women would bring potato salad and that sort of thing. Sometimes we had to eat in the cars if the dust was bad, but we would spend an afternoon. And I remember my mother and dad just moving from car to car, sitting with friends, visiting, and maybe visiting with somebody else. And it was a great afternoon—of no shade. If it was a hot day, people still came."

Despite losing his house and his hardware store to the Depression, Trixie's father had decided to start again, this time in the farm implement business. Like other Dust Bowl merchants, he innovated to find ways to lure potential customers to town: "The Chamber of Commerce planned a lot of events that were free. My dad had movies, free movies. They were movies that John Deere furnished, not Hollywood movies, advertising more than anything else. But they were free. And Dad would have pop. And everybody would come. It would get people to town. There were just a lot of events that were free that people could participate in—get people to town, hoping that they can use their cream and egg money and buy a pair of shoes." (Caroline Henderson noted the allure of such events: "A local implement agency recently sent out invitations to a tractor entertainment with free moving pictures of factory operation and the like," she wrote, without naming the town or the merchant. "The five hundred free lunches prepared for the occasion proved insufficient for the assembled crowd.")

Attracting people with free movies and pop, however, did not mean they could afford to buy new farm equipment. Despite everything Trixie's father did to bring in customers, this business, too, soon foundered. The pressure, Trixie said, mounted steadily on him:

We had a cow in the back lot. He milked every morning, every evening, and he always got up before five o'clock. It was still dark always. And he was out milking one morning, and he was so distressed, so nervous because a representative from John Deere was going to be there that day to pick up a check for some piece of machinery. And he did not have the money. He had used it for something else.

In the Texas Panhandle, a weary Nettie Featherston (below, left, in a flour sack dress) waits for rain near Childress. In Follett, Trixie Travis Brown's father opened a John Deere dealership (below).

Drifting dirt blown from neighbors' abandoned fields became a growing concern to those farmers who remained—like the ones in Guymon, Oklahoma (above), and near Dalhart, Texas (right), where giant dunes had formed.

While he was milking he collapsed. And when he woke up he was under the cow. He was looking at the sky. It was full of stars. And he said, "I decided that nothing is worth having this much anxiety. This will work out. I'll never do this again."

He had a workshop in the back of the store, a repair shop. And I believe that we survived on the repairs, because farmers did not quit planting; they didn't quit trying to work their land. Those who stayed were gamblers and optimistic, and each year they would think that it was going to be better. They couldn't afford his new equipment. So I believe that it was his repair shop that kept us afloat. And somehow or another it worked out.

FOR THOSE TRYING DESPERATELY to hold on to their land, the constant work of keeping their own fields from being swept away and of attempting to eke out some crop, however paltry, was hard enough.

But now they faced another threat that only added to their troubles: the 9 million abandoned acres of bare fields—an area larger than the state of Maryland—spread across the southern Plains.

Any progress farmers might make on stabilizing their own land, Caroline Henderson complained, was too quickly "buried by the smothering silt from the fields of rugged individualists who persist in their right to do nothing." She had particular contempt for the "suitcase farmers" who had plowed up so much soil, but lived far away from the crisis they had helped create.

"The land takes a lot of care, and there's people that just don't take care of it," Floyd Coen explained. "There were farmers that just got up and left, and of course that field would just blow away. You just don't go off and leave this bare ground to the elements to move it around, cause you're gonna get wind here and it'll sure move it around."

In some cases, the absentee owners would enlist farmers who had remained to tend the abandoned fields. Boots McCoy's

Urge Martial Law In The 'Dust Bow

Desperate Appeal Is Made
The President In Dramatic
tempt To Control Increas
Devastation Now Prevalent

A meeting of farmers and busi
men from Kansas, Texas and Okl
ma, was held in Guymon, Okla
April 22nd and after considerable
cussion a united action was deter
ed upon to call upon the Fed
Government for the establishmen

Farmers (like those in Texas, above, left) became so desperate for help in making absentee owners and negligent neighbors take care of their fields, they called for martial law to be imposed (above).

father, for one. "Dad would get the mail," Boots said, "and read me a postcard from somebody that owned some land, saying, 'Mr. McCoy, if you farm our land, if there's any money made, well put our part in the bank either at Guymon or at Elkhart or at Clayton.' Dad would farm three thousand acres of wheat at one time." Though not yet even in his teens, Boots was expected to help out: "We'd drive them old tractors. And as a kid my cousin and I both had belts made for us, where they could chain us onto a tractor and we couldn't fall off so we could drive a tractor. We worked just like men."

The steady exodus of landowners, however, meant the problem seemed to keep growing. "Nothing that you see or hear or read will be likely to exaggerate the physical discomfort or material losses due to these storms," Caroline Henderson wrote. "Land once owned and occupied by farm families is now passing into ownership of banks, mortgage companies . . . and investment partnerships or corporations.

The legal notices published in our county paper for the past week include two notices of foreclosure proceedings and nine notices of sheriff's sales. . . . These eleven legal actions involve the ownership of 3,520 acres of land."

The farmers who had adopted soil scientist Howard Finnell's advice found themselves at the mercy of those who hadn't. This, historian Donald Worster said, created a conundrum that challenged some of their core beliefs:

> *If one man mishandled his land, everybody suffered under these conditions. All it took was one thousand-acre farm blowing dirt badly to disrupt the lives of everybody around him, to disrupt their pastures, to disrupt their fields and crops, to make their livestock suffer. So it became a problem of how do you control one another under these circumstances? What do you say to your neighbor down the line? What do you say to him to make him stop?*

There was no culture here of mutual coercion, mutually agreed on. Everybody was out there for himself to begin with. And if that farm operator actually happened to be living in Amarillo or Denver and only came out on weekends anyway, who did you talk to? There was no authority to stop this sort of process.

In April, farmers from five states met in Guymon and called upon the federal and state governments for more financial assistance to carry out the conservation work Finnell had been advocating. "The problem in the 'Dust Bowl' is entirely too large for the remaining good farmers to even make a start to cope with," they wrote. "[We] must have help and it's imperative [we] have help now."

More than that, they also wanted every landowner to be required to leave stubble on harvested fields, and they wanted some way to make sure abandoned acres were planted with cover crops. To do it, they called for the establishment of a Dust Bowl Authority—modeled on the new Tennessee Valley Authority in the Southeast—with broad powers to enforce regulations. (Another group called for the outright elimination of "nonresident operators.")

They even suggested that martial law be declared to mobilize an army of tractors and listers to go to work on "every square foot of blowing land" whether the owner of the land agreed or not. It was a radical idea, fueled by "extreme desperation," according to historian Pamela Riney-Kehrberg: "I think it has to be pretty extreme for a group of farmers, very independent-minded, very stubborn, a group that on the whole doesn't like to be meddled with, to say, 'Please come and meddle with us.' But at this point they're into their sixth year of no income, their fifth year of no crops, and they're seeing neighbors' fields blowing into their own. They're seeing enormous clouds of dirt in the air, and they don't know what else to do. And when you don't know what else to do and you're afraid of losing your farm, then you begin to ask for rather more extreme measures than you would have asked for otherwise."

"When your back is against the wall, all ideology goes out the window," added Worster. "So here is a group of people who are very anti-state, anti-government, who never wanted the government interfering with anything they did or telling them what to do, but who, when the chips are down, are going to ask for the only help they can get—and that's from the federal government."

The antipathy against too much government interference was still strong, and governors of the southern Plains states

A banner in Texas announces what's at stake on the southern Plains, even if "destroyed" is misspelled (below, right); a telegram from the new conservation district in Perryton to an absentee owner in Oklahoma City is more direct (below): if he doesn't take care of his land, they will—and place a lien on it for the expense.

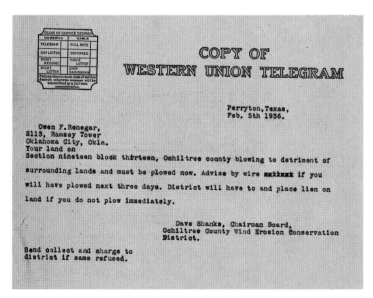

refused to declare martial law. But the legislatures passed laws setting up soil conservation districts, meant to devise and enforce better farming practices through consensus. Kansas permitted counties to adopt "soil drifting" resolutions that imposed fines on landowners who refused to follow conservation practices; in Haskell County, farmers were even granted the right to enter a neighbor's field and work on it to prevent the soil from blowing.

And while the federal government decided against a Dust Bowl Authority, it allocated another $1.7 million in emergency payments (75 cents per acre) to farmers for carrying out wind erosion work: knocking down the dunes, chiseling into the hardpan, and then plowing along the contour with the old-fashioned lister before planting crops that might hold the soil in place. And doing it again and again after every storm, if necessary.

Floyd and Dale Coen went to work on some of the toughest parts of Morton County, Kansas. "You couldn't drive a tractor over these sand humps because it would turn the tractor over," Floyd said. "It'd be steep enough on one side that the tractor just went backward, so you had to put two tractors on a cable or a chain or something and kind of saw through the mounds." Dale added, "We just took railroad irons that were fifteen, twenty feet long and tied chains on each end of the tractor and just went back and forth across those humps of sand and dirt. And you would just drag off a little every time you went across until you finally got it leveled off. By just continually circling around and comin' back over it and over it and over it and get it to where it was leveled down pretty well."

Imogene Davison Glover's father resented having the government telling him how to farm, but he took the incentive

ol. LIII   Number 30

No Payments Unless Land Tilled Right

Eighty-Five Percent of Land Must Be Worked To Entitle Operator To Participate in Program; Will Pay for Weed Growth

New rulings issued this week by the AAA require that 85 per cent of crop land must be farmed before a person

Farmers were induced into following new techniques by getting government payments for their conservation work, as *The Elkhart Tri-State News* reported in July 1937 (opposite, top). They sometimes needed bulldozers—and help paying for the gasoline—to knock down the big dunes (opposite, bottom), before they could begin contour plowing (above).

money and did the work, she said: "He didn't agree with the government on anything. But he did try to plow or farm according to their specifications so the dirt wouldn't blow. He'd have done anything to keep that dirt from blowin' away. They had him plow in sort of circles instead of straight because the wind would just whip those straight furrows level. And if they kind of banked it and did what they called soil conservation, he thought that was smart."

From Wayne Lewis's perspective, once farmers saw that the methods worked, "we didn't have to have a program to tell us to do it. Just as soon as we could afford to buy the chisels, we did that and broke the ground up." And Caroline Henderson considered it a point of pride to make sure people understood that she and Will were not the reason the new programs were needed. "We did not wait ourselves for the government or anyone to tell us to go to listing our own fields to control as far as possible the blowing and loss of surface soil," she wrote. "We feel that to some extent it has been helpful in holding our own acreage this far. But to be genuinely effective, such a plan must be carried out on a large scale and not left to piecemeal efforts."

Farmers now got help to buy gasoline for their tractors, if they were doing soil erosion

work, and they received payments from the Soil Conservation Service to plant soil-conserving grasses and feed crops, instead of wheat. In Cimarron County, Oklahoma, the average farm took in $4,000 in government aid. Just to the north, the agent in Morton County, Kansas, reported that federal support payments were the only income source in the region, and compliance was 100 percent.

For government officials, Donald Worster said, the problem boiled down to, "We have got to begin to induce people to plant less. How do you do that? You can't just take their land away from them. So the idea was to pay them not to produce. For the people in the Great Plains this was a salvation. They could keep their land, they didn't have to go out every fall and plant wheat again; the government would send them a check, and year after year this could go on and until better times emerged."

Agricultural historian R. Douglas Hurt considers the moment a turning point in American farm policy:

Nobody knew whether any of this would really work or how long it would take. It might be fifty years, it might be seventy years, and nobody knew, although they bandied those terms about.

It's an age of great experimentation. Basically the officials and the scientists and the farmers and the agricultural groups ultimately decided that the only way to control this problem is to limit production. The only way you could limit production, given the independent nature of farmers, is to pay them to limit production.

And for the remainder of the twentieth century this is the great problem in agricultural policy. But in the 1930s the federal government and farmers are dealing with this issue really for the first time. And it's the first time that you really have a federal intervention into agriculture that in some respects one could call a planned economy.

But had there not been this drought and had there not been this plow up of the southern Plains which came together in a moment of time, who can say whether the federal government would be such an active participant in agriculture as it is today. I think it's a time period in which the federal government entered agriculture as never before—and it's never left.

Howard Finnell's studies had convinced him that nearly 20 percent of the land under cultivation was submarginal—not suited for crops. Those acres, he recommended, should be reseeded with native grasses. To make sure that happened, the government continued buying back as much as it could from dusted-out farmers.

In 1937, the Agriculture Department asked for $10 million to buy nearly 2 million acres and permanently turn them back to grassland. Some 786,250 acres were purchased in southeastern Colorado and 161,644 acres in northeastern New Mexico. The government also bought 92,836 in Morton County, Kansas, and a combined 288,678 acres in Dallam County, Texas, and 85,452 acres in Cimarron County,

Oklahoma. (They would later become the Comanche, Kiowa, Cimarron, and Rita Blanca National Grasslands, respectively, part of a larger system now administered by the U.S. Forest Service.)

The program explicitly prohibited the government from forcing landowners to sell, but locals—except those who felt fortunate to find any buyer at all and happily made the transaction and moved on—routinely criticized it. It took too much land off the property tax rolls, they said, and it reminded them too much of the earlier talk coming out of Washington about deliberately depopulating the Plains. Because of the opposition, the land purchases were terminated in a few years.

Just as he believed parts of the southern Plains should return to its natural state, Finnell was equally sure that most of it, the remaining 80 percent of the cultivated fields, could become productive again, if farmers followed his suggestion to focus as much on their soil as they did on the weather:

It is hard for the Plains farmer to see repeatedly what is manifestly drought injury to the crops and not send up a cry for more rainfall.

Since better use of the same rainfall would have the same effect as an increased amount, it is a pertinent fact that under some conditions as much as four-fifths of the rainfall never reaches the subsurface and subsoils where it may be drawn upon by crops. In such cases, additional rainfall is much less needed than agricultural practices which make more efficient use of that which falls.

The experiments in his demonstration projects had provided Finnell with a rough formula for predicting success, based on the amount of moisture present in the soil at the time of planting. When the moisture penetrated less than 2 feet, half of the sowed wheat failed completely; where moisture was present 3 feet or more

In "Operation Dust Bowl," Howard Finnell's team took a series of photographs of a field covered with dunes (opposite, top right) and the progress that was made in leveling them (opposite, top left) that ultimately resulted in a restored rangeland (opposite, bottom).

TEX 1251 G

from the surface, no crops failed, and more than three-quarters of the acres returned respectable harvests. Finnell's programs of summer fallowing and contour plowing all showed that fields treated that way captured more of the precious precipitation and let it sink deeper into the soil. Where that didn't happen, he advised the farmers to plant something else. Convinced by the data, some banks announced they would not make loans on wheat if the soil 2 feet below the surface of a farmer's field was dry at planting time.

Finnell's biggest challenge was north of Dalhart, the heart of "Operation Dust Bowl." There, more than 2,000 acres were covered with sand dunes. One 470-acre field had 57 of them, the largest 880 feet long and 36 feet high. "If we cannot stabilize them with some practical covering of vegetation," Secretary of Agriculture Henry Wallace had said about those dunes and others like them, "they will grow larger, join together, smother great areas of useful land, and perhaps become altogether unmanageable." Finnell's team tackled them with bulldozers and heavy equipment—and a method called a "wind intensifier," which turned the force that had created the dunes into something that helped reduce them. Grasses better suited to sandy soils, including some brought back

by government scientists from the deserts of Africa, were planted to hold the newly landscaped fields in place.

In a series of photographs taken over the course of eighteen months, Finnell showed how dunes that once towered above one of his employee's cars had been tamed and turned into a productive pasture. And the contrast between contoured fields that retained the rain versus those farmed the old way was striking. One farmer even complained that terracing created wet spots where his tractor bogged down—though he had to admit it also increased his wheat yields.

With such tangible results, more and more farmers decided to follow Finnell's advice. By the end of 1937, despite the persistent dust storms, the amount of dangerously eroded land had been reduced by more than half. Caroline Henderson gave credit to Finnell and the New Deal:

> People here . . . realize that the benefit payments [from the Soil Conservation Service] and the wage payments from the federal work projects are all that have saved a large territory here from abandonment.
>
> There seems no doubt that improved methods of tillage and protection

By the beginning of 1938, Howard Finnell's theories were getting more attention (above). The signal for Pauline Heimann Robertson's family to return from Kansas to their ranch in New Mexico was when the Russian thistles grew again (opposite and above, right), although the scene of devastation awaiting them was startling. For a while, they harvested the thistles and ate them.

are already yielding some results in reducing wind erosion.

That there was anything at all to harvest we attribute to the new planting methods encouraged by the Soil [Conservation] Service of listing on contour lines and laying up terraces.

Then, in 1938, the rainfall edged upward—more than 18 inches in Boise City—and although the number of dust storms receded only slightly, some farmers in No Man's Land brought in a wheat crop of 10 bushels per acre. Nothing close to a bumper crop, but almost bountiful compared to previous years. The mayor of Hooker, Oklahoma, asked local businesses to let some of their employees help out with the harvest and ease a temporary labor shortage created because so many farmers had left. At one of Howard Finnell's demonstration projects, land that had sold for $8 an acre in 1935 was now worth four times as much.

Pauline Heimann Robertson's father had promised his family that when there was enough rain for the Russian thistles, he would move them all back from central Kansas to their ranch in New Mexico. Now he kept that promise. ("Daddy didn't have no give-up," Pauline explained.)

"We were tickled to death to come home," she said, "but when we got there it was sad. The dirt would be blowin' up around the house up to the eaves. The grass was blown. There was no vegetation. But those thistles—in a drop of rain a thistle will grow a little, and that's kind of the way it did." As the family tried to get back on its feet in their old home, the thistles became more than a symbol of the signal for their return, she said:

We ate those thistles. We picked those thistles when they were tender; if they get too big you can't do that. Mother was with us, and she'd tell us which area to pick. And we would pick a great big panful, because when you cook 'em, they cooked down, and you don't have as many.

But there's so much food value in those thistles for the livestock as well the human. It's like spinach, really. And so we just we ate that.

BACK IN 1935, WHEN HE WAS NINE years old and looked up the canyon walls where he and his family lived in Union County, New Mexico, Sam Arguello had been the first to see the approach of the devastating Black Sunday storm. Three years later he saw something equally frightening: a horde of approaching grasshoppers.

"They were crawlers really," he said. "They weren't even hopping yet. And they came down the canyon wall in solid sheets. When they got down to the bottom, we had some chickens out there at the ranch house, and the chickens, boy they went crazy. They had grasshoppers! But before you knew it, the chickens took off and went to the roost in the chicken house and got away from 'em, 'cause the whole ground was moving. I mean just solid, clear across. It was as horrible as a dust storm, except that it was on the ground instead of in the air. It was horrid."

Having scared off the chickens, the hoppers advanced on the Arguello family's big garden. "The grasshoppers came in that evenin', and by next mornin' there was nothin' but just the hard stalks left out there," he said. "Everything was gone. My folks used to raise some real hot little chili peppers and they were all eaten. There was nothin' but the stems there. The cucumbers were gone. The watermelon was gone. Tomatoes. Everything. Just cleaned out."

The ground was so thick with bugs that when young Sam rode his horse to get the mail or some groceries, he said, "you'd pull up on the reins and the horse would slide on the grasshoppers. And that's a fact. That's not make-believe. I went through it. I know it."

After counting the number of grasshoppers under a few of his watermelons, one farmer made an estimate of the infestation on his land: it was 23,400 grasshoppers per acre; 14 million per square mile. Another man spread some luminous paint on the grasshoppers moving through his land, in hopes of tracking their speed as they crawled along. Eight hours later, they were 2½ miles away.

"They were moving steadily east," Arguello remembered. "The whole ground was moving, everything. It was just solid." As they climbed up out of the canyon where his family lived, "they had to go around the rocks and up there. And you could look up on the hillside between the rocks where they had cleaned out all the grass in between the rocks. And they kept on goin'. And what I understand is, somewhere in Oklahoma they grew wings. And they all took flight. And they said they shaded the sun cause they were all together."

Survivors talked of thinking a cloud was on the horizon, except that as it got closer they heard it buzzing and realized it was a cloud-sized swarm of grasshoppers. Any recently planted grass disappeared; the insects even ate the wooden handles on pitchforks. "You know," Lorene Delay White said, "we began to think, 'Could anything more go wrong?' "

Farmers hooked up sleds to their tractors and dragged them across the fields, trapping grasshoppers in vats of kerosene. Some tried crushing them under rollers. Several states called out their National Guard to help CCC workers and highway departments spread poison, mixed with sawdust and molasses and banana oil, along the roadsides. In Sam Arguello's Union County alone, they used 19,555 gallon drums of poison and 176 boxcars loaded with sawdust.

"They mixed up big vats of poison," Timothy Egan said, "and they went out and sprayed it out all over this land. How much more out of whack could the land itself be? By the time they were pouring poison on the land, poison on land that had been killed by them, I think they had gone so far down the road in altering this great grassland that it was almost beyond repair."

Some stretches of highway became dangerously slick from the dead bugs. "Well, they killed 'em," Sam said. "And then when we had rains, the creeks, water holes, our swimmin' holes were black. Black, full of grasshoppers."

To combat the invasion of grasshoppers (opposite), farmers dragged sleds across their fields to trap them (top) or spread poison to kill them (middle), resulting in large piles of dead bugs (above). The National Guard and CCC were called in to help.

Chapter 12

THE WESTERN GATE

Don't believe all you may hear or read about any striking "comeback" of the Dust Bowl. Conditions in general are really somewhat better; there is more feed, better cover, and some fair looking wheat where it was sown immediately after the September rain.

But the rich native grasses of our earlier days are gone forever, and we are, at best, years removed from anything like a full recovery. Some cling to the idea that the dust-blowing is over, but I'd rather wait until March or April or early summer to make a prophecy.

We know that there is all around us much bare, untilled land ready to blow whenever the wind rises. So we shall have to wait and see.

—Caroline Henderson

ON JULY 11, 1938, A TRAIN bearing President Franklin Delano Roosevelt pulled into the station at Amarillo, Texas, the largest city in the Dust Bowl, making his first official tour of the southern Plains. In honor of his visit, organizers had assembled what they claimed to be the world's largest marching band: 3,000 people—anyone, they said, between the ages of nine and ninety who could play "The Eyes of Texas" on any instrument.

For weeks in advance, another group had gathered at the Red Cross headquarters in town, sewing 130 yards of red, white, and blue material into an American flag 22 feet high and 49 feet wide—the "biggest flag ever seen in the Panhandle," according to the *Amarillo Daily News*—to display for the president they believed hadn't given up on them.

"All of the Democrats were excited," Pauline Durrett Robertson said. "There were people in Amarillo who did not like Roosevelt, and they were usually the wealthy people. I know one of them, one of the rich men I heard say, 'This socialistic regime is not American. It's anti-American.' Those of us who were poor appreciated the programs that Roosevelt started." Pauline's father, whose business and health had failed in the Depression and whose wife

had suffered a mental collapse, "was really glad that he had a chance to see and hear this man in person," Pauline said, "because he admired him and he admired what he had tried to do for the people in trouble."

An estimated crowd of 200,000—four times the population of the city itself—turned out, according to the local newspaper, lining the 3-mile route of Roosevelt's motorcade to Ellwood Park, where he was helped to the podium by his son, Elliott, and began to speak:

> *I wish that more people from the South and the East and the Middle West could visit the Plains country. If they did you would hear less talk about the great American desert, you would hear less ridicule of our efforts to conserve water, to restore grazing lands and to plant trees.*
>
> *Back in the East, in Washington and on the Hudson River, I have seen the topsoil of the Panhandle and of western Kansas . . . borne by the high wind in the air . . . to the Atlantic Ocean itself. I want that sight to come to an end.*
>
> *People who are ignorant and people who think only in terms of the moment*

In 1938, Pauline Durrett Robertson's father (opposite, with one of her sisters) was among the huge crowd in Amarillo that turned out to hear President Roosevelt (above and right, with his son, Elliott) offer words of encouragement. It rained that day, a shower that FDR called "a mighty good omen."

Preceding pages:
Rain clouds return and loom over a vast Texas landscape.

Fields plowed using Howard Finnell's methods (above) captured the returning rain and reduced the scope of the Dust Bowl. In New Mexico, Pauline Heimann Robertson and her brother (left) went back to rounding up cattle.

scoff at our efforts and say, "Oh, let the next generation take care of itself—if people out in the dry parts of the country cannot live there let them move out and hand the land back to the Indians."

But my friends, that is not your idea or mine. We seek permanently to establish this part of the nation as a fine and safe place which a large number of Americans can call home.

Every year that passes we are learning more and more about the best use of the land, about the conserving of our soil and the improvement of it by getting everything we can out of every drop of water that falls from the heavens—and today is a good example of it.

Just then, it began to rain. "And it's an old-fashioned gully washer," said Timothy Egan. "And the rain comes off of Roosevelt's spectacles and he continues—he's got his clamped knees up there and he continues to give his speech, 'I'm never going to desert you.' And they're straining to hold this giant American flag, and then the colors start to leak out. And you can see the colors of the flag leaking into the gutter in the rain."

"We had been wishing for rain, praying for rain; it rained and still there was a big crowd," Pauline Durrett Robertson remembered. "It rained the day he came," she repeated, smiling, "so he took credit for that."

"I think," the president concluded, that "this little shower we have had is a mighty good omen." Then his motorcade drove back up the rain-washed streets, and Roosevelt boarded his train and left.

Later that year, Robert Geiger of the Associated Press interviewed Howard Finnell about the progress being made in "Operation Dust Bowl" and the prospects for the coming year. "We can't say those days [of dust] are gone forever," Finnell answered, "but next spring southwestern skies should be less dusty than any spring since 1932."

Some precipitation in early 1939 brought a glimmer of hope, which grew when the Soil Conservation Service announced that, thanks to better farming practices, the soil was in its best condition in seven years. But the storms weren't over. One black blizzard in March covered 100,000 square miles, and a return of dry weather ruined the harvest in many counties.

Still, by the end of the year, the Dust Bowl had shrunk to one-fifth its previous size. Throughout the region, people noticed the change in different ways.

Pauline Heimann Robertson and her family had already moved back home to Union County, New Mexico, once her father had determined there was enough moisture for the Russian thistles to thrive. But they were wary of setting their hopes too high. "We kept thinking, as dry as it got and how it all happened, you didn't know for certain how long this rain was gonna be coming," she said. "But I don't know how many weeks, we'd get a little rain and a little rain. And I remember that when it first started, the sunflowers started growin'. They were in our pasture that was close to the house. When we went to get our milk cows, which we did on horseback, you had to hunt 'em 'cause you couldn't see 'em. The sunflowers would be up above our head on the horse."

In Follett, Texas, Trixie Travis Brown's father, who had gone through two business losses as a merchant in town, had been trying to persuade his wife to pull up stakes and move to Idaho, to land he had already scouted out:

My mother was very reluctant because all of her family—probably fifty people of the four hundred and thirty-seven in Follett were all relatives. She just was not willing to say yes.

My father had the whole move planned; he even had the land picked out in Idaho. He had the map out. And mother just kept holding out.

Dad had leased a half-section of what was good farmland [near Follett]—that would be three hundred and twenty acres—and planted wheat. He was somewhat of a gambler in that he was willing to take chances.

We plant in September. In April, when the wheat was getting high, we had a late storm. It was a heavy snowstorm; one of our school buses was not able to get the children home. And all the men in the city were out all night trying to get that bus out of drifts and get those children delivered. But that

The improved conditions meant that Trixie Travis Brown's family shelved its plans to emigrate to Idaho, allowing her to stay at Follett High School, where she was the drum majorette (below, in white hat, front row, second from left) and sports reporter (below, right).

TRIXIE TRAVIS
SPORTS REPORTER

snow nourished our wheat, our three hundred and twenty acres like you can't believe.

We began to go out on a regular basis. Mother and Dad liked to take drives anyway. Mother got so worn out with all the kids in the house that she would say, "George, let's take a drive out to look at the wheat."

We would go out and stand and see how high it was to us children. We'd stand there and they'd sort of measure the height of the wheat. And then when it began to really develop, it was obvious it was going to be a really good wheat crop. And it was. And the prices were good. And that's what gave my dad a start.

The map went into a drawer—and the trip to Idaho was cancelled.

Slowly, things began improving. The rains became more frequent and better timed for the growing season. "No one will ever know what it meant to us to have it rain," Lorene Delay White said. "That's what we prayed for, what we yearned for,

was the rain that came that would soak into the ground and let us raise a crop and eventually stop the dust."

For Lorene's neighbors in southwestern Kansas, the Coens, the rains were a welcome sight. "When it did start raining it was such a blessing," Floyd Coen said. "We'd go out in the rain and hold our hands up and let that hit our hands and our face. And we just almost worshipped that rain, because we knew then that we were going to have some crops. One in particular I remember. There was water standing everywhere; I'd never seen anything like that. We must have had three or four inches of rain. And we'd just go out and walk through those mud holes—I don't think I ever got down and wallowed in 'em, but you just wanted to be a part of it. You knew that good was going to come from the whole thing."

Down in No Man's Land, near Caroline and Will Henderson, Imogene Davison Glover said, "It just seemed happier everywhere you went. Everybody, not just my folks, but when we'd go to the neighbors we always felt like things were better. And I remember the first year that we probably

The *Boise City News* deployed big words and a map (below and bottom) to proclaim better times. Edgar and Rena Coen's family (below, left) grew bigger and more prosperous.

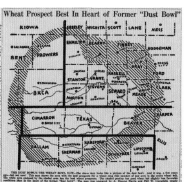

Panhandle Drops Pernicious "Dust Bowl" Cognomen

Wildcats Lose To Beaver Grid Squad

Locals Complete Conference Contest In Second Place

The "Dust Bowl" has officially vacated Texas and the Panhandle of Oklahoma, according to the Amarillo News of Wednesday.

Improved conditions—more moisture during the past several years notwithstanding the present dry condition, good cover crops and better soil cultivation and conservation practices—have forced Old Man Wind to withdraw farther north if he is going to find any loose soil to blow up for his annual spring duststorms.

The so-called "Dust Bowl" still exists but right now and for the coming year or so it will be con-

Wheat Prospect Best In Heart of Former "Dust Bowl"

The return of the rains brought the return of the wheat and a return of smiling faces. In 1940, most farmers made money from their crop for the first time in ten years.

had a good crop after the Dirty Thirties, we got stuck in the field, and Daddy didn't even gripe about it, he was so glad that we were havin' rain."

Nearby, at his farm in the Oklahoma Panhandle, Dorothy Sturdivan Kleffman's father decided it was now safe to bring his wife and children back from Arkansas:

> They had a saying here that if you wear out a pair of boots here in the Panhandle, you'll come back. And as soon as he got some land under control then he moved us all back.
>
> And when we did come back, the land had been recovered, they had learned how to terrace the land. And I remember my dad had a wheat crop I think in 1940 that was a good wheat crop. It was a bountiful wheat crop, and we thought, "We're back. We survived."

By 1940, the drought that had gripped the southern Plains for nearly a decade was officially over. That year, many farmers harvested their first profitable crop since 1930. In the hard-hit southwestern corner of Kansas, which had witnessed the greatest exodus and farm abandonment during the last ten years, the agricultural agent declared: "Morton County can no longer be called the Dust Bowl."

> December 13, 1944. We had for once a super-abundance of rain and already three snows. . . . Wheat was a fair crop. We saved most of it between rains. I worked on [the] combine or tractor through both harvests. But much of the rich barley was lost by the over-whelming growth of sunflowers.
>
> We had ample pasturage with the increased rainfall and cattle have done reasonably well. The Leghorns have paid house bills and a good part of the farm expenses, and we had a nice garden with most of our winter's living stored away.

—Caroline Henderson

JUST AS IT HAD THIRTY YEARS earlier, the outbreak of a world war in Europe and the return of a relatively wet weather cycle brought prosperity to the southern Plains.

The wet cycle of the 1940s sometimes created pooled water on the Henderson homestead (top, right), but both Caroline (above) and Will (top, left) were in their seventies and the hard work was taking its toll.

Wheat prices skyrocketed and harvests were bountiful. A farmer who had yielded products worth $1,000 in the 1930s might now expect nearly $12,000.

By 1945, Caroline Henderson could report; "We have at last assembled most of the materials for piping water into the house with a [sink] in the kitchen and indoor toilet in the bathroom. But we need a Superman to do the work." Later, she noted, "We have both worn down fast during the years of extreme desolation since 1931. Every small accomplishment now seems to demand a greater output of energy and resolution than in the years that are gone."

Caroline was grateful for better weather and higher prices, but she and her husband, Will, were now nearing seventy. She suffered from asthma; he had a heart condition—and neither of them could forget the stern teachings of the Dust Bowl. "It is good to remember that the laws of the universe recognize no favorites and cherish no hostility or small vindictiveness," she wrote. "That before sun and rain, stormy winds, or summer's kind beneficence, we all stand upon one common level."

But reliable rains and bumper crops made it difficult for many others to feel such humility toward "the laws of the universe." In the first five years of the 1940s, land devoted to wheat expanded by nearly 3 million acres, as speculators and "suitcase farmers" returned. Parcels that had sold for $5 an acre during the Dust Bowl now commanded prices of $50, $60, sometimes $100 an acre. "You can't make me believe we've learned our lesson so it will stick," a Kansas farmer said. "It's just not in our blood to play a safe game."

After a reunion of the Last Man Club in Dalhart (John L. McCarty had already moved on to take a job with the bigger Amarillo newspaper), the *Dalhart Texan* mockingly offered a $50 reward for "information leading to proof of authorship of the term Dust Bowl." Some of the recently formed conservation districts cancelled their agreements with the Soil Conservation Service so they could plow up reseeded rangeland. "I always said I was the only one who could remember those dreadful days, for any practical purpose," Caroline confided to a friend. "People have simply assumed it couldn't happen again."

In 1946, Howard Finnell warned that

more than half of the land being turned to wheat fields was in sections the Soil Conservation Service had classified as unsuitable for cultivation. Even some of the shelterbelts of trees established during the dry years were being torn out to plant wheat:

> *The old familiar routine is being faithfully carried out. During an hour's drive into the countryside . . . there were twenty-nine powerful tractors to be seen ripping up the sod.*
>
> *They were plowing again the land reclaimed from the dust by government help and sowed back to grass in the 1930s. They were also turning over native sod on shallow soils never before plowed.*

Overplowing in the 1940s contributed to the "Filthy Fifties" (below) when a two-year drought returned.

> *If this situation is any different from that of the late 1920s, it is worse. . . . The same process is starting again in the very same place.*

Then, in the early 1950s, the wet cycle ended and a two-year drought replaced it. The storms picked up once more. Donald Worster's parents had returned from California to western Kansas by now. He was in grade school at the time and lived through events that would later help him understand the much larger catastrophe of the Dust Bowl as an environmental historian: "About ten o'clock in the morning, the entire sky turned completely dark. It was like seven or eight o'clock at night. The teachers came into all the classrooms and said, 'We're sending you home. Go home as fast as you possibly can.' So we took off running

down these alleys and streets toward home. By the time I got home, which was before noon, the dust had settled all over the part of town I lived in. It was inside the house. You could feel the dirt inside the house. You couldn't see much around you because the dirt was so thick. When we got up the next morning and opened the icebox, and it was an old-fashioned icebox, dirt was inside the refrigerator. That one was a short-lived event. It only lasted for about twelve hours. But in the 1930s those kinds of conditions went on in some cases for days, even weeks at a time."

Bad as the "Filthy Fifties" were, the drought didn't last as long as the "Dirty Thirties." The damage to the land was mitigated by those farmers who continued using Howard Finnell's conservation practices. And because nearly 4 million acres of submarginal land had been purchased by the government during the Dust Bowl and permanently restored as national grasslands, the soil didn't blow as much. At least a few lessons had been learned.

But now, instead of looking to the skies for rain, many farmers began looking beneath the soil, where they believed a more reliable—and irresistible—supply of water could be found: the vast Ogallala aquifer, a huge underground reservoir stretching from Nebraska to north Texas, filled with water that had seeped down for centuries after the last Ice Age. With new technology and cheap power from recent natural gas discoveries in the southern Plains, farmers could pump the ancient water up, irrigate their land, and grow other crops like feed corn for cattle and pigs that require even more moisture than wheat.

To many of those who lived through the Dust Bowl—and those who have studied its history closely—this seems as much of a folly as the Great Plow Up. "The only thing that's holding that ground together is that irrigation water that comes out of the Ogallala," said Charles Shaw. "The Ogallala is about a hundred feet deep on the average. We've used over fifty feet of it now. We've got about twenty years of water left under portions of these eight states and it's disappearing. Now, there's no way you

can save the land without the water and continue to farm it. If you lose the water you're gonna lose the land. And that's it in a nutshell. The lesson of the Dust Bowl is that it's going to blow away if you don't concede to its needs. You've got to adapt yourself to it. It's not gonna adapt to you."

"The Ogallala Aquifer is depleting, we know we are mining this water," according to Donald Worster. "I think the Dust Bowl can happen again; most emphatically can happen again. The Great Plains are perhaps the most vulnerable part of the United States in an age of global warming. It can become a creeping Sahara. The Sahara Desert a few thousand years ago was a savannah. We know that it's possible to turn from savannah to a stark desert and there's no reason to think that it can't happen in the middle of North America.

"The Dust Bowl belongs on the list of the top three, four, five environmental catastrophes in world history. But those took place over hundreds and even thousands of years of deforestation. We created a world-class environmental disaster in a matter of forty or fifty years. That we could do it so quickly and so ruthlessly is a hard thing to take into our moral imagination." (The other disasters ecologists rank with the Dust Bowl include the destruction of vegetation by livestock in the Mediterranean region and the deforestation of China's uplands around 3000 B.C.)

Timothy Egan calls the Dust Bowl "a classic tale of human beings pushing too hard against nature and nature pushing back. And then it's a classic American bubble story too, like stocks and like real estate. We think that everything that goes up will not come down, that we can defy gravity—and that's what we did here."

To Calvin Crabill, the lesson of the Dust Bowl is simple. "It's a very good lesson for us today: Take care of the environment or it will do us in." His cowboy father learned it the hard way, reluctantly helping plow up the grasslands and then being driven from the land when it turned on him.

Wayne Lewis's parents remained and ultimately prospered. "My folks put in one

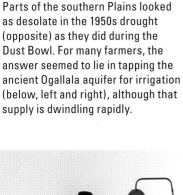

Parts of the southern Plains looked as desolate in the 1950s drought (opposite) as they did during the Dust Bowl. For many farmers, the answer seemed to lie in tapping the ancient Ogallala aquifer for irrigation (below, left and right), although that supply is dwindling rapidly.

For Caroline Henderson (in her garden in the 1950s, opposite) the lessons of the Dust Bowl were clear: work hard, stay out of debt, and adjust to the "great silent unseen forces of Nature." She and Will (at right on a rare picnic) refused to use irrigated water from the Ogallala aquifer, or to allow an absentee management company to manage the land once they left their homestead in the 1960s (opposite, below).

of the first irrigation wells and we thought it was a great idea," he said. "As I look back at it now, it was the beginning of a bad idea. Having irrigation water permitted us to do some things that weren't good for the long term. And some of these days I'll be gone but somebody is gonna be out of water. I think that someday down the road folks are gonna have trouble getting enough drinking water. And they'll look back and say, 'And to think back there in the Fifties and Sixties they used up our drinking water to raise hog feed.'"

Lewis understands the human impulses that propelled the Great Plow Up and the mining of the Ogallala's underground waters, but as a former wheat farmer and science teacher in his mid-nineties, he said that human impulses aren't always meant to be followed: "We want it now—and if it makes money now it's a good idea. But if the things we're doing are going to mess up the future, it wasn't a good idea. Don't deal in the moment. Take the long-term look at things. It's important that we do the right thing by the soil and the climate."

"History," he added, "is of value only if you learn from it."

August 1, 1965. Another hot and desolate day. . . . We are both quite weakened by our struggles, either with asthma or a desperate cough, I believe largely the result of working with the dusty wheat. . . .

Am still quite weak and don't gain strength as I'd like to, but manage to carry out the routine work of the home and help as I can with outdoor tasks.

We had reason to hope for a good rain for the feed crop—just now in need of encouragement, but the moisture was cut off with only a light shower.

—*Caroline Henderson*

ON HER HOMESTEAD IN NO MAN'S Land, Caroline Henderson carried on without resorting to irrigation water from the Ogallala aquifer. She questioned whether "even our apparently unfailing supply of deep groundwater could stand the drain of continuous pumping" and worried that while "the supplies of gas under the Panhandle can be utilized to develop cheap power for pumping . . . [h]ere again we come up against the hard fact that every material resource comes to an end unless constantly replenished."

It had been nearly sixty years since she first arrived on the southern Plains, full of dreams of farming her own land and prospering from its bounty. In that time, she and Will had seen only ten bumper crops—and oftentimes she expressed feelings of failure to those she knew best.

As they approached the age of eighty, they were still using the farm equipment they had purchased in the 1920s, because Caroline would not borrow money for land or machinery. Although electricity had reached the homestead in 1952, she wouldn't even buy a fan to combat the summer heat, considering the expense an extravagance. But they were free of debt; their daughter

had become a successful doctor and had given them a grandson with a bright future.

In her old age, Caroline steadfastly refused to turn her land over to a farm management company—"strangers," she called them, "of some faraway money-gathering corporation with no possible interest in this small bit of the 'good earth.'"

In 1965, with both of them in bad health, she finally agreed to go to Arizona to live with their daughter. They returned to No Man's Land the next spring for a final visit. Will died three days later. Caroline joined him, passing through what she called "the western gate," within a few months.

In accordance with her wishes, the homestead was placed in trust—on the condition that it never be plowed again.

To prepare the ground as well as we may, to sow our seeds, to cultivate and care for, that is our part. Yet how difficult it is for some of us to learn that the results we must leave to the great silent unseen forces of Nature, whether the crop be corn or character.

—*Caroline Henderson*

ACKNOWLEDGMENTS

THIS BOOK AND THE FILM THAT ACCOMPANIES it were collaborative projects that required a great number of people, as Caroline Henderson put it, "to prepare the ground as well as we may, to sow our seeds, to cultivate and care for." Now that harvesttime has arrived, we'd like to thank them, though they are far too many to name here or in the film credits printed elsewhere. But thank them, we do. All of them.

In particular we'd like to express our deepest gratitude to the more than two dozen survivors of the Dust Bowl who so generously shared their childhood memories with us—some extraordinarily painful, all remarkably fresh and vivid three-quarters of a century after the fact. Their names recur throughout the preceding pages, just as their images and voices do throughout our documentary. They ranged in age from the mid-eighties to late nineties when they sat down in front of our cameras to tell their families' stories three years ago, and a handful of them have already passed through "the western gate" before our film and book were finally finished. We were honored to meet them and hope that the larger narrative we have woven does justice to each one of them by extending their generosity to a larger audience and preserving their stories for future generations.

Julie Dunfey, our fellow producer, and associate producer Susan Shumaker were responsible for finding these witnesses of history. Without their hard work, resourcefulness, and repeated visits to the heart of the former Dust Bowl, this project would have been a pale shadow of what it became: perhaps the last major effort to record the living testimony of the survivors of that extraordinary time, before sheer actuarial arithmetic leaves none left to tell its tales. Holding round tables at local historical societies, talking with officials at nursing homes and senior centers, sifting through letters sent in response to public service announcements placed in local newspapers and on area PBS stations, and using simple, old-fashioned journalistic shoe leather, Julie and Susan eventually talked with several hundred survivors for potential interviews. From those, we eventually settled on the people who animate our narrative.

During their search, Julie and Susan, in turn, found friendly assistance from a multitude of sources, including: Debbie Colson at the No Man's Land Historical Museum in Goodwell, Oklahoma; Jody Risely and Phyllis Randolph at the Cimarron Heritage Center in Boise City, Oklahoma; Jacque Swanner at the Jones and Plummer Trail Museum in Beaver, Oklahoma; Victoria Baker of the Herzstein Museum in Clayton, New Mexico; and Nicky Olson at the XIT Museum in Dalhart, Texas. A number of local PBS stations and people working for them were incredibly helpful, as well: Linda Pitner, Lynne Groom, and Jackie Smith of KACV in Amarillo; John McCarroll, Lori Holliday, and Ashley Barcum of OETA in Oklahoma City; Sally Stowe and Bryan Shadden at KVIE in Sacramento; Donna Sanford and Pam Osborne of Rocky Mountain PBS in Denver; Jane Habiger of Smoky Hills Public Television in Kansas; KERA in Dallas, KTWU in Topeka, and KPTF in Wichita.

Associate producer Aileen Silverstone, aided by Jim Pontarelli, Susan Shumaker, and Katelynn Vance, unearthed more than six thousand photographs to help bring our story to life, many of them never before made public. To find them, they traveled to Oklahoma, Kansas, Texas, Colorado, and New Mexico, as well as the National Archives and Library of Congress in Washington, D.C. Julie Dunfey, with the help of Katy Haas, amassed hours' worth of archival footage—old newsreels, government films, and a few home movies—that demonstrated the kinetic fury of black blizzards and sandstorms in motion, as well as their devastating aftermath. The interviews were beautifully filmed by Buddy Squires (who also shot the atmospheric scenes of abandoned farmhouses and the sweeping Plains) and Steve McCarthy.

Then our editing team took over for a year and a half to put it all together as a film: editors Craig Mellish and Ryan Gifford; assistant editors Meagan Frappiea and Richard Rubin; apprentice editor Katy Haas; technical director Dave Mast. The same talented team did the sound effects and the post-editing finishing work on all the images. All the while, other members of the Florentine Films family in Walpole, New Hampshire, kept the project moving on schedule: Elle Carriére, Brenda Heath, Patty Lawlor, and Chris Darling.

We feel fortunate to have had a distinguished group of advisers to look over early scripts, attend a number of screenings of the film in progress, and offer their suggestions on how to make our narrative not only accurate but more powerful: Paul Barnes, Sarah Botstein, Tim Clark, Timothy Egan, Pauline Hodges, R. Douglas Hurt, William E. Leuchtenburg, David McMahon, Lynn Novick, Pamela Riney-Kehrberg, Geoffrey C. Ward, and Donald Worster.

We can't think of anyone better than Peter Coyote to narrate our script, nor anyone better than Carolyn McCormick to inhabit the words of Caroline Henderson. The equally talented Patricia Clarkson, Amy Madigan, and Kevin Conway rounded out our small cast of voices. As always, we relied on Bobby Horton and Jacqueline Schwab to provide additional musical arrangements and performances to our soundtrack—playing everything from Woody Guthrie tunes to old hymns.

We are grateful to our funders, who made this project possible by their financial support: Bank of America, the Arthur Vining Davis Foundations, the Rockefeller Foundation, the Wallace Genetic Foundation, the Dana A. Hamel Family Charitable Trust, Robert and Beverly Grappone, the National Endowment for the Humanities, the Public Broadcasting Service, and the Corporation for Public Broadcasting. And we also wish to thank our friends at our producing partner, WETA-TV in Washington, D.C.—Sharon Rockefeller, David Thompson, Dalton Delan, Jim Corbley, Craig Impink, Anne Harrington, and many others; Joe DePlasco and his team at Dan Klores Communications; and Mac Talmadge for his design help.

For this book, we thank our agents, Jennifer Rudolph Walsh and Jay Mandel of William Morris Endeavor Entertainment; our editor, Sarah Malarkey, of Chronicle Books; and designer Suzanne LaGasa.

For everything else, and much more, we thank our families: Dianne, Emme, and Will Duncan, and Julie, Sarah, Lilly, Olivia, and Willa Burns. One of the powerful themes in the story of the Dust Bowl is the importance of families in providing refuge (emotional as well as physical) and stability in the darkest, most turbulent times, binding people together, as Caroline Henderson said, "by memory and hope." Memory and hope. We thank our wives and children for providing both in great abundance.

DAYTON DUNCAN
KEN BURNS
Walpole, New Hampshire

SELECTED BIBLIOGRAPHY

IN THIS BOOK AND FILM PROJECT WE HAVE RELIED more heavily than any we have ever done on the oral histories of the people who lived through a particular moment in American history rather than on the subsequent scholarship about that moment. Nonetheless, to construct the narrative framework and place it in a larger context, we have consulted the extensive library—academic and popular—about the Dust Bowl that has built up over nearly eighty years.

First and foremost are the works of the historians who served as advisers to our film and appeared in it. In addition to what they told us on camera and the advice they gave us in the editing room, they were invaluable in having written the best and most important books to date about the topic. We referred to those books constantly and recommend them highly: Donald Worster's *Dust Bowl: The Southern Plains in the 1930s*; Timothy Egan's *The Worst Hard Time*; Pamela Riney-Kehrberg's *Rooted in Dust*; and R. Douglas Hurt's *The Dust Bowl: An Agricultural and Social History*.

Alvin O. Turner's wonderful edition of Caroline Henderson's *Letters from the Dust Bowl* not only provides the eloquent writings of an intelligent and indomitable woman in one volume; it also breathes vivid life into the person behind the words. Similarly, Douglas Wixson's edition of Sanora Babb's reports and letters (and her sister Dorothy's photographs) shines a much-needed light on a remarkable yet little known woman whose personal story is as fascinating as the ones she wrote.

For information about soil scientist H. Howard Finnell—government reports, speeches, newspaper and magazine articles—we are grateful to his descendants, Joseph and Myrna Finnell, and to Oklahoma State University's collection of the Finnell papers. Linda Coen Passmark kindly shared her history of the Edgar and Rena Coen family; Charles Shaw let us have access to "Sunshine and Shadows," the unpublished reminiscence of his mother, Hazel Lucas Shaw.

We are thankful for the help from the Cimarron Heritage Museum in Boise City, Oklahoma, the Morton County Historical Society in Elkhart, Kansas, and the XIT Museum in Dalhart, Texas, for providing reams of information, especially back copies of the *Boise City News*, the *Dalhart Texan*, and the *Amarillo Daily News*. We looked through many other local newspapers in our research, received a number of letters and pamphlets from people with stories to share about their (or their parents') time in the Dust Bowl, and pored over scores of government bulletins and reports—all too many to name here.

What follows, then, is not an exhaustive bibliography but a list of the principal sources we turned to throughout the process of making our film and this book:

Babb, Sanora. *On the Dirty Plate Trail: Remembering the Dust Bowl Refugee Camps.* Ed. Douglas Wixson. Austin: University of Texas Press, 2007.

Bennett, Hugh Hammond. *Soil Conservation.* New York: McGraw-Hill, 1939.

Bonnifield, Paul. *The Dust Bowl: Men, Dirt, and Depression.* Albuquerque: University of New Mexico Press, 1979.

Brink, Wellington. *Big Hugh: The Father of Soil Conservation.* New York: Macmillan, 1951.

Cunfer, Geoff. *On the Great Plains: Agriculture and Environment.* College Station: Texas A&M Press, 2005.

Dawson, John C. *High Plains Yesterdays: From XIT Days Through Drouth and Depression.* Austin, Texas: Eakin Press, 1985.

Egan, Timothy. *The Worst Hard Time: The Untold Story of Those Who Survived the Great American Dust Bowl.* Boston: Houghton Mifflin, 2005.

Ganzel, Bill. *Dust Bowl Descent.* Lincoln: University of Nebraska Press, 1984.

Gregory, James N. *American Exodus: The Dust Bowl Migration and Okie Culture in California.* New York: Oxford University Press, 1991.

Guthrie, Woody. *Bound for Glory.* New York: E. P. Dutton, 1943.

Henderson, Caroline. *Letters from the Dust Bowl.* Ed. Alvin O. Turner. Norman: University of Oklahoma Press, 2001.

Hendrickson, Kenneth D., Jr. *Hard Times in Oklahoma: The Depression Years.* Oklahoma City: Oklahoma Historical Society, 1983.

Hurt, R. Douglas. *The Dust Bowl: An Agricultural and Social History.* Chicago: Nelson-Hall, 1981.

Johnson, Vance. *Heaven's Tableland: The Dust Bowl Story.* New York: Farrar, Straus, 1947.

Kennedy, David M. *Freedom From Fear: The American People in the Depression and War, 1929–1945.* New York: Oxford University Press, 1999.

Klein, Joe. *Woody Guthrie: A Life.* New York: Alfred A. Knopf, 1980.

Leuchtenburg, William E. *Franklin D. Roosevelt and the New Deal.* New York: Harper & Row, 1963.

Lookingbill, Brad D. *Dust Bowl USA: Depression America and the Ecological Imagination, 1929–1941.* Athens: Ohio University Press, 2001.

Lowitt, Richard. *The New Deal and the West.* Norman: University of Oklahoma Press, 1984.

Lowitt, Richard, and Maurine Beasley, eds. *One-Third of a Nation: Lorena Hickok Reports on the Great Depression.* Urbana: University of Illinois Press, 1981.

Nelson, Paula M. *The Prairie Winnows Out Its Own: The West River Country of South Dakota in the Years of Depression and Dust.* Iowa City: University of Iowa Press, 1996.

Nichols, David, ed. *Ernie's America: The Best of Ernie Pyle's 1930s Travel Dispatches.* New York: Random House, 1989.

Nixon, Edgar B. *Franklin D. Roosevelt & Conservation 1911–1945.* Washington, D.C.: Government Printing Office, 1957.

Reisner, Marc. *Cadillac Desert: The American West and Its Disappearing Water.* New York: Viking-Penguin, 1987.

Riney-Kehrberg, Pamela. *Rooted in Dust: Surviving Drought and Depression in Southwestern Kansas.* Lawrence: University Press of Kansas, 1994.

Riney-Kehrberg, Pamela, ed. *Waiting on the Bounty: The Dust Bowl Diary of Mary Knackstedt Dyck.* Iowa City: University of Iowa Press, 1999.

Saloutos, Theodore. *The American Farmer and the New Deal.* Ames: Iowa State University Press, 1982.

Sears, Paul. *Deserts on the March.* Norman: University of Oklahoma Press, 1935.

Stein, Walter J. *California and the Dust Bowl Migration.* Westport, Connecticut: Greenwood Press, 1973.

Svobida, Lawrence. *An Empire of Dust.* Caldwell, Idaho: Caxton Printers, 1940.

Vestal, Stanley. *Short Grass Country.* New York: Duell, Sloan & Pearce, 1941.

Watkins, T. H. *The Great Depression: America in the 1930s.* Boston: Little, Brown, 1993.

–*The Hungry Years: A Narrative History of the Great Depression in America.* New York: Henry Holt, 1999.

Webb, Walter Prescott. *The Great Plains.* New York: Grosset & Dunlap, 1931.

Worster, Donald. *Dust Bowl: The Southern Plains in the 1930s.* New York: Oxford University Press, 1979.

Wunder, John R., Frances W. Kaye, and Vernon Carstensen, eds. *Americans View Their Dust Bowl Experience.* Boulder: University Press of Colorado, 1999.

Yurchenco, Henrietta. *A Mighty Hard Road: The Woody Guthrie Story.* New York: McGraw-Hill, 1970.

The Black Sunday dust storm of April 14, 1935, moves from Elkhart, Kansas, toward the small town of Rolla, passing over the Coen family farm and the cemetery where they had buried Rena Marie and Dwayne.

PHOTO CREDITS

ENDSHEET Wolf Creek Heritage Museum

PREFACE National Archives and Records Administration

PREFACE Panhandle-Plains Historical Museum, Canyon, TX

PREFACE Green Family Collection

PREFACE Carson County Square House Museum, Panhandle

CONTENTS Historic Adobe Museum, Ulysses, KS

PAGE 14 National Archives and Records Administration

PAGE 16 The Library of Congress, Prints & Photographs Division

PAGE 19 Getty Images

CHAPTER 1 Harpers Ferry Center, Historic Photo Collection

PAGE 23 TOP LEFT: Eleanor Grandstaff Collection TOP RIGHT: Eleanor Grandstaff Collection BOTTOM: Eleanor Grandstaff Collection

PAGE 24 Kansas State Historical Society

PAGE 25 LEFT: Cimarron Heritage Center RIGHT: Geraland Bond

PAGE 26 TOP: Cimarron Heritage Center BOTTOM: Cimarron Heritage Center

PAGE 27 Imogene Davison Glover

PAGE 28 TOP LEFT: The Coen Family Collection TOP RIGHT: The Hazel and Clarence Beck Family Collection BOTTOM: The Hazel and Clarence Beck Family Collection

PAGE 29 No Man's Land Historical Museum, Goodwell, OK

PAGE 30 Historic Adobe Museum, Ulysses, KS

PAGE 31 LEFT: Crabill Family Collection RIGHT: Forester Family Collection

PAGE 32 Eleanor Grandstaff Collection

PAGE 33 LEFT: *The Boise City News* RIGHT: Cimarron Heritage Center

PAGE 35 TOP: Eleanor Grandstaff Collection BOTTOM LEFT: *Atlantic Monthly* BOTTOM RIGHT: Eleanor Grandstaff Collection

PAGE 36 Stanley G. Crump

PAGE 37 Institute for Regional Studies, NDSU, Fargo, ND

PAGE 38 TOP: Getty Images/*Life* Magazine BOTTOM: Lewis Family

PAGE 39 Ida Watkins Collection

CHAPTER 2 Gary Hanna Collection

PAGE 42 McCoy Collection

PAGE 43 Gary Hanna Collection

PAGE 44 TOP: Panhandle-Plains Historical Museum, Canyon, TX BOTTOM: Corbis

PAGE 45 LEFT: Lorene Delay White RIGHT: National Archives and Records Administration

PAGE 46 LEFT: Eleanor Grandstaff Collection RIGHT: *The Boise City News*

PAGE 47 LEFT: Lucas-Shaw Photo Collection RIGHT: Cimarron Heritage Center

PAGE 48 Historic Adobe Museum, Ulysses, KS

PAGE 49 LEFT: Historic Adobe Museum, Ulysses, KS RIGHT: *The Boise City News*

PAGE 50 XIT Museum, Dalhart, TX

PAGE 51 TOP: Meade County Historical Society BOTTOM: Historic Adobe Museum, Ulysses, KS

PAGE 52 The Library of Congress, Prints & Photographs Division

PAGE 54 LEFT: Carson County Square House Museum, Panhandle, TX RIGHT: Corbis

PAGE 55 TOP: Getty Images BOTTOM: National Archives and Records Administration

PAGE 56 TOP: *The Boise City News* BOTTOM: *The Boise City News*

PAGE 57 Scott County Historical Society

PAGE 58 Research Division of the Oklahoma Historical Society

PAGE 59 LEFT: The Travis Family RIGHT: Dorothy Sturdivan Kleffman

PAGE 60 TOP: Research Division of the Oklahoma Historical Society BOTTOM LEFT: Crabill Family Collection BOTTOM RIGHT: Ina K Roberts Labrier

PAGE 61 Historic Adobe Museum, Ulysses, KS

CHAPTER 3 Cimarron Heritage Center

PAGE 65 TOP: Franklin D. Roosevelt Library and Museum BOTTOM: *Gastonia Daily Gazette*

PAGE 66 Getty Images

PAGE 67 LEFT: *The Boise City News* RIGHT: Research Division of the Oklahoma Historical Society

PAGE 68 TOP: Dorothy Sturdivan Kleffman BOTTOM: Getty Images

PAGE 69 Margaret Bourke-White Papers, Special Collections Research Center, Syracuse University Library

PAGE 70 The Travis Family

PAGE 71 LEFT: Pauline Hodges Collection RIGHT: The Travis Family

PAGE 72 LEFT: Millard Fowler Collection RIGHT: Millard Fowler Collection

PAGE 73 TOP: Lucas-Shaw Photo Collection BOTTOM: *The Boise City News*

PAGE 74 TOP: XIT Museum, Dalhart, TX BOTTOM: Lucas-Shaw Photo Collection

CHAPTER 4 National Archives and Records Administration

PAGE 78 Research Division of the Oklahoma Historical Society

PAGE 79 LEFT: Kansas State Historical Society RIGHT: Associated Press

PAGE 80 TOP LEFT: Forester Family Collection TOP RIGHT: The Library of Congress, Prints & Photographs Division BOTTOM: *The Boise City News*

PAGE 81 LEFT: Associated Press RIGHT: Larry and LaDonna Meyers

PAGE 82 Associated Press

PAGE 83 Corbis

PAGE 84 LEFT: Lorene Delay White RIGHT: Lorene Delay White

PAGE 85 The Coen Family Collection

PAGE 86 TOP: The Coen Family Collection BOTTOM: The Coen Family Collection

PAGE 87 Morton County Historical Society

CHAPTER 5 Associated Press

PAGE 90 TOP: Lucas-Shaw Photo Collection BOTTOM: Lucas-Shaw Photo Collection

PAGE 91 TOP: Associated Press BOTTOM: Associated Press

PAGE 92 The Travis Family

PAGE 93 TOP: The Library of Congress, Prints & Photographs Division BOTTOM: Sam Arguello Family

PAGE 94 TOP: The Ed Stewart Family BOTTOM LEFT: The Ed Stewart Family BOTTOM CENTER: The Ed Stewart Family BOTTOM RIGHT: The Ed Stewart Family

PAGE 95 Amarillo Public Library

PAGE 96 Historic Adobe Museum, Ulysses, KS

PAGE 97 LEFT: McCoy Collection RIGHT: Historic Adobe Museum, Ulysses, KS

PAGE 98 LEFT: Lucas-Shaw Photo Collection RIGHT: Norma Gene Young Collection

PAGE 99 Kansas Heritage Center, Dodge City

PAGE 100 LEFT: Forester Family Collection RIGHT: *Miami Daily News-Record*

PHOTO CREDITS, CONTINUED

PAGE 170 The Harry Ransom Center, The University of Texas at Austin

PAGE 171 LEFT: The Harry Ransom Center, The University of Texas at Austin RIGHT: The Library of Congress, Prints & Photographs Division

PAGE 172 LEFT: The Library of Congress, Prints & Photographs Division TOP RIGHT: The Library of Congress, Prints & Photographs Division BOTTOM RIGHT: © The Dorothea Lange Collection, Oakland Museum of California. Gift of Paul S. Taylor

PAGE 173 TOP: The Harry Ransom Center, The University of Texas at Austin BOTTOM LEFT: Seth Pace Collection BOTTOM RIGHT: The Library of Congress, Prints & Photographs Division

PAGE 174 LEFT: Courtesy of the Woody Guthrie Archives TOP RIGHT: © Woody Guthrie Publications, Inc. & Tro-Ludlow Music, Inc. (BMI). Courtesy of the Woody Guthrie Archives BOTTOM RIGHT: Courtesy of the Woody Guthrie Archives

PAGE 175 TOP LEFT: The Hazel and Clarence Beck Family Collection TOP RIGHT: Forester Family Collection BOTTOM: Forester Family Collection

PAGE 176 LEFT: Crabill Family Collection RIGHT: Crabill Family Collection

PAGE 177 TOP LEFT: The Harry Ransom Center, The University of Texas at Austin TOP RIGHT: The Harry Ransom Center, The University of Texas at Austin BOTTOM: The Harry Ransom Center, The University of Texas at Austin

PAGE 178 LEFT: Viking Press RIGHT: The Harry Ransom Center, The University of Texas at Austin

PAGE 179 LEFT: Seth Pace Collection RIGHT: Seth Pace Collection

CHAPTER 11 National Archives and Records Administration

PAGE 183 TOP LEFT: Eleanor Grandstaff Collection TOP RIGHT: Eleanor Grandstaff Collection BOTTOM: Eleanor Grandstaff Collection

PAGE 184 TOP LEFT: Morton County Historical Society TOP RIGHT: Morton County Historical Society BOTTOM: Morton County Historical Society

PAGE 185 TOP: Research Division of the Oklahoma Historical Society BOTTOM: Research Division of the Oklahoma Historical Society

PAGE 186 LEFT: The Library of Congress, Prints & Photographs Division RIGHT: The Boise City News

PAGE 187 TOP: Associated Press BOTTOM: Carson County Square House Museum, Panhandle, TX

PAGE 188 LEFT: Virginia Kerns Frantz RIGHT: The Boise City News

PAGE 189 Ginger Roach Collection

PAGE 190 LEFT: The Library of Congress, Prints & Photographs Division RIGHT: The Travis Family

PAGE 191 LEFT: The Library of Congress, Prints & Photographs Division RIGHT: XIT Museum, Dalhart, TX

PAGE 192 LEFT: The Library of Congress, Prints & Photographs Division RIGHT: The Elkhart Tri-State News

PAGE 193 LEFT: Natural Resources Conservation Service, Perryton, TX RIGHT: The Library of Congress, Prints & Photographs Division

PAGE 194 TOP: The Elkhart Tri-State News BOTTOM: National Archives and Records Administration

PAGE 195 Research Division of the Oklahoma Historical Society

PAGE 197 TOP LEFT: Panhandle-Plains Historical Museum, Canyon, TX TOP RIGHT: Panhandle-Plains Historical Museum, Canyon, TX BOTTOM: Panhandle-Plains Historical Museum, Canyon, TX

PAGE 198 LEFT: Research Division of the Oklahoma Historical Society RIGHT: The Library of Congress, Prints & Photographs Division

PAGE 199 LEFT: The Boise City News RIGHT: The Library of Congress, Prints & Photographs Division

PAGE 200 TOP: National Archives and Records Administration CENTER: The Library of Congress, Prints & Photographs Division BOTTOM: Kansas State Historical Society

PAGE 201 Corbis

CHAPTER 12 The Library of Congress, Prints & Photographs Division

PAGE 204 Robertson-Durrett Family Photos

PAGE 205 TOP: Panhandle-Plains Historical Museum, Canyon, TX BOTTOM: Franklin D. Roosevelt Library and Museum

PAGE 206 LEFT: Pauline Heimann Robertson RIGHT: Research Division of the Oklahoma Historical Society

PAGE 207 LEFT: Stanley G. Crump RIGHT: Wolf Creek Heritage Museum

PAGE 208 LEFT: The Coen Family Collection TOP RIGHT: The Boise City News BOTTOM RIGHT: The Boise City News

PAGE 209 LEFT: Museum of the Great Plains, Lawton, OK RIGHT: The Library of Congress, Prints & Photographs Division

PAGE 210 LEFT: Eleanor Grandstaff Collection TOP RIGHT: Eleanor Grandstaff Collection BOTTOM RIGHT: Eleanor Grandstaff Collection

PAGE 211 Getty Images/Life Magazine

PAGE 212 Getty Images/Life Magazine

PAGE 213 LEFT: Associated Press RIGHT: Associated Press

PAGE 214 TOP: Eleanor Grandstaff Collection BOTTOM LEFT: Eleanor Grandstaff Collection BOTTOM RIGHT: Eleanor Grandstaff Collection

PAGE 215 Eleanor Grandstaff Collection

PAGE 216 Eleanor Grandstaff Collection

PAGE 217 Eleanor Grandstaff Collection

PAGE 220 Tarrant Family Collection, courtesy of Anthony DiGiusti

PAGE 227 Kansas State Historical Society

PAGE 232 Eleanor Grandstaff Collection

ENDSHEET Research Division of the Oklahoma Historical Society

DUSTJACKET FRONT Associated Press BACK Carson County Square House Museum, Panhandle, TX

FILM CREDITS

Directed by
Ken Burns

Written by
Dayton Duncan

Produced by
Dayton Duncan
Ken Burns
Julie Dunfey

Edited by
Craig Mellish
Ryan Gifford

Associate Producers
Aileen Silverstone
Susan Shumaker

Cinematography
Buddy Squires
Stephen McCarthy

Narrated by
Peter Coyote

Voice of Caroline Henderson
Carolyn McCormick

Other Voices
Patricia Clarkson
Kevin Conway
Amy Madigan

Assistant Editors
Richard Rubin
Meagan Frappiea

Technical Director
Dave Mast

Apprentice Editor
Katy Haas

Program Advisers
Paul Barnes
Sarah Botstein
Tim Clark
Timothy Egan
Pauline Hodges
R. Douglas Hurt
William E. Leuchtenburg
David McMahon
Lynn Novick
Pamela Riney-Kehrberg
Geoffrey C. Ward
Donald Worster

Chief Financial Officer
Brenda Heath

Associate Financial Officer
Patty Lawlor

Coordinating Producer
Elle Carrière

Assistant to the Director
Christopher Darling

VP for Development
Kim Klein

Additional Cinematography
Allen Moore

Assistant Camera
John Romeo
Jill Tufts
Rod Williams

Sound Recording
Francis X. Coakley
Doug Dunderdale
John Osborne
Marl Roy

Research Associate
Katelynn Vance
Jim Pontarelli
Stephanie Houle

Research Assistant
Polly Pettit

Production Assistants
Nick Belloni
Aidan Daniell
Christi Mitchell
Lisa D. Olken
Bill Perry
E. J. Sanders
Alison Victor
Derek Watson

Dialogue Editor
Craig Mellish

Sound Effects Editors
Ryan Gifford
Dave Mast
Meagan Frappiea

Music Editor
Craig Mellish

Assistant Sound Editor
Katy Haas

Sound Post-Production
Sound One

Re-Recording Mixer
Dominick Tavella

Voice-Over Recording
Lou Verrico
Cityvox, New York
Rob Dickson
Command Productions,
Sausalito, California

Digital Image Restoration and Animation
Richard Rubin
Meagan Frappiea

Animated Maps
Richard Rubin

HD Finishing Services
Goldcrest Post

HD Colorist
John J. Dowdell III

HD Finishing Artist
Peter Heady

HD Finishing Supervisor
Tim Spitzer

Film Dailies
Du Art Film Labs

Archival Film Transfer
Colorlab
Deluxe

Legal Services
Drew Patrick
Robert N. Gold
Valerie Marcus

Instrumentalist and Studio Arrangements
Bobby Horton

Traditional Music
Jacqueline Schwab, piano

Music Recorded at
Soundesign Recording,
Brattleboro, Vermont

Music Engineers
Billy Shaw
Alan Stockwell

Transcription Services
Colleen Sackheim

Graphic Design Consultant
Mac Talmadge

Interns
Daehyun An
Evan Barlow

Johnny Bassett
James Boehmer
Dan Callahan
Máximo Dell'Oliver
Carl Elsasser
Justin Foreman
Emma Frankel
Chris Greene
Peter Haubrich
Erin Heinert
Jeffrey Holmes
Laura Hopkins
Stephanie Houle
Lindsay Jackson
Ethan Kamer
Clare Keating
Ryker Kelvin
Carlene Kucharczyk
Meredith Helene Lackey
Amanda Lundquist
Adnelly Marichal
Emily Maysilles
Stephen Miceli
Rory Moon
Emma Mullen
Anne Munger
Taylor Nagel
Hunter Nichols
Nicole Perry
Tina Rapp
Ben Savard
David Schmidt
Chris Synder
Natalie Thomson
Katelynn Vance

Funding Provided by
Bank of America
Public Broadcasting Service
Corporation for Public Broadcasting
National Endowment for the Humanities
The Arthur Vining Davis Foundations
Rockefeller Foundation
Wallace Genetic Foundation
The Better Angels Society, including the Dana A. Hamel Family Charitable Trust, and Robert and Beverly Grappone

AFTER THE DUST BOWL

SAM ARGUELLO served as a U.S. Marine in the Pacific during World War II and then had a successful career as manager of a regional lumber company. He was also one of the best broncobusters in the Texas and Oklahoma panhandles.

CLARENCE BECK put himself through college, served in the Army Air Force during World War II, and then found work as an engineer, focusing on the nuclear propulsion of atomic submarines. He received several awards and patents, eventually becoming a millionaire many times over. He died in the spring of 2011.

LOUISE FORESTER BRIGGS has been a spiritual seeker her entire life—as a Presbyterian elder, a participant in New Age programs, and a teacher of "A Course in Miracles." She retired after touching the lives of hundreds of students up and down the West Coast and now lives in Nevada.

TRIXIE TRAVIS BROWN earned a master's degree in teaching and literature, then put her husband Jack through dental school, and kept her family of five fed by selling cemetery plots. She retired to travel the world, before settling down on a hilltop overlooking Monterey, California.

DALE COEN served in Europe during World War II as part of the Army Air Force. He raised wheat and cattle in Morton County, Kansas, but found his calling in the Community of Christ, where he ministered to congregations in Colorado and Kansas for more than 50 years. He lives in Elkhart, Kansas.

FLOYD COEN is a successful rancher and farmer in Morton County, Kansas. He has served in the Kansas State Legislature and received several statewide honors, including the Distinguished Jayhawker award and the Distinguished Service to Agriculture award. Floyd and his wife Maxine were recognized by the State of Kansas with the Master Farmer and Homemaker Award.

CALVIN CRABILL became a naval navigator during World War II, then attended UC Berkeley on the GI bill, having first worked in the animation department at Walt Disney Studios. He taught high school and college math for more than 30 years and authored three best-selling textbooks, one of which is still used today.

ROBERT FORESTER worked in Sequoia National Park's Giant Forest before serving in the Korean War and completing a master's degree in education—a degree he put to use as a teacher and school counselor for more than 30 years. He retired to the Napa Valley, where he lives in a beautiful four-acre setting with his wife Betty.

WILLIAM FORESTER served in the Korean War in communications intelligence in Japan. He received his BA from UC Berkeley and then began a lifelong career in teaching, implementing the first personal computer labs in Bay Area schools. After retiring, he moved to a hilltop overlooking Ashland, Oregon.

MILLARD FOWLER became a prosperous farmer in Cimarron County, Oklahoma, acquiring more than three sections of irrigated land and renting several hundred acres more. He owned two profitable Boise City businesses, as well—a ready-mix concrete plant and, with his brother, a successful welding shop. He retired from farming at age 95.

VIRGINIA KERNS FRANTZ had seven children before enrolling at Oklahoma Panhandle State University in 1966 and earning her teaching degree. She spent 22 years in the classroom, as a teacher at Guymon High and as a student, receiving a master's degree in counseling.

IMOGENE DAVISON GLOVER was a "Rosie the Riveter" during World War II, raised a family of three, and had successful careers in journalism, teaching, and real estate. Proud of her Depression-era roots, she named her agency "Dust Bowl Real Estate" and kept its doors open until 2009.

IRENE BECK HAUER graduated from Van Nuys High in California, a schoolmate of Jane Russell and Marilyn Monroe. During World War II, she ran a drill press at Lockheed Aircraft. After retirement, Irene traveled the country with her husband, Max.

PAULINE ARNETT HODGES holds a PhD in education and has taught in schools and colleges in Oklahoma, Kansas, and Colorado. A reading specialist, she authored four groundbreaking textbooks and implemented successful reading programs in 49 states.

DOROTHY STURDIVAN KLEFFMAN was the 1942 valedictorian of Guymon High School. During the war, she worked as a telephone operator in town. She later married, raised a family, worked as an accountant and school cook, and was the first female elder in her church. She died in January 2011.

INA K ROBERTS LABRIER left teaching in 1938 to marry a local rancher. Together, they owned and worked nearly 12 square miles of ranchland, running cattle and riding the range together. Today, the property is a dude ranch, run by Ina K's daughter. Nearing age 100, Ina K still helps in the kitchen.

WAYNE LEWIS graduated from Friends University with a degree in chemistry and devoted his life to teaching—in his hometown community of Gate, Oklahoma, and in Holtville, California. After retirement, he built his own solar-powered home. He died in March 2012.

ROBERT "BOOTS" MCCOY became a successful farmer and rancher, at one time owning the second largest wheat farm in Oklahoma and running more than 5,000 head of cattle. He also owned racehorses and served as a municipal judge. At home, he still drives a tractor and heats his home with wood he's cut himself.

SHIRLEY FORESTER MCKENZIE married and set up housekeeping just a block from her parents' home on Heather Ridge Way in Oakland. There she raised two sons and lived for 38 years before retiring in the Pacific Northwest, after working as a nurse, a receptionist, and a traveling typist, driving around the Bay Area in a pale blue Thunderbird.

TEX PACE, who'd once lived in a government camp himself, managed a series of labor camps in the Central Valley before opening an insurance agency specializing in agriculture. A girl he met at a government camp became his wife of more than 70 years.

PAULINE DURRETT ROBERTSON was Amarillo High School salutatorian and graduated summa cum laude from Amarillo College. She worked as an accountant, raised 10 children, and then started Camp Friendship, a summer program for under-privileged children of all ethnicities.

PAULINE HEIMANN ROBERTSON and her husband purchased a ranch adjoining her parents' in Union County, New Mexico, running 1,500 head of cattle and raising vegetables, chickens, and turkeys. On weekends, the family drove to the First Baptist Church of Clayton—60 miles each way—where she taught Sunday school and played the piano during services. She died in July 2011.

CHARLES SHAW followed in his father's footsteps and became a mortician. An inaugural teacher in the nation's first degreed mortuary science program, Charles eventually returned to Vici, Oklahoma, and took over the family business.

DON WELLS spent two years in the Army and served as an instructor at West Point. He returned home to Cimarron County, Oklahoma, and became a successful farmer and businessman, owning a grain elevator and several thousand acres of land. In 2005 he retired as a self-made millionaire.

LORENE DELAY WHITE graduated from Elkhart High School, taught school, owned a dress shop, and eventually settled down to ranching, farming, and raising a large family. In the fall of 2009, she was named Pioneer Woman of Morton County, Kansas, in recognition of her successful life on the southern Plains.

DOROTHY CHRISTENSON WILLIAMSON, a Phi Beta Kappa graduate of Colorado College, met her husband Howard while serving in rural Prowers County as a social worker. They moved to Denver, where, at age 99, Dorothy still lives in the same home—and still tackles the *New York Times* crossword puzzle each morning.

A Kansas farmer in the midst of a seemingly hopeless task: using a shovel to attack the sand drifts that have buried his fields and his equipment.

INDEX

Page numbers in italics indicate photographs.

This page:

The windmill at Caroline Henderson's homestead, 1960s.

Endsheet image:

A black blizzard descends on Hooker, Oklahoma, June 4, 1937.

Food Store

THE MODEL

CARL MERCANTILE CO.

● Dorothy Williamson

● Calvin Crabill

Colorado

SPRINGFIELD ■

New
Mexico

● Sam
Arguello

● Ina K Labrier

Millard Fowler
Charles Shaw
● The   ■
Becks   BOISE CITY

Don Wells

CLAYTON ■

Pauline Heimann ●
Robertson

DALHART ■

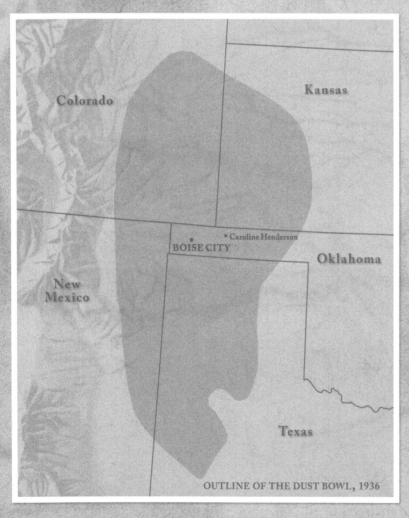

Colorado

Kansas

■ * Caroline Henderson
BOISE CITY

Oklahoma

New
Mexico

Texas

OUTLINE OF THE DUST BOWL, 1936